Eric Voegelin

LIBRARY OF MODERN THINKERS

PUBLISHER: T. KENNETH CRIBB JR.
SERIES EDITOR: JEFFREY O. NELSON

PUBLISHED TITLES

ROBERT NISBET *by Brad Lowell Stone*

LUDWIG VON MISES *by Israel M. Kirzner*

WILHELM RÖPKE *by John Zmirak*

ERIC VOEGELIN *by Michael P. Federici*

FORTHCOMING

MICHAEL OAKESHOTT *by Timothy Fuller*

BERTRAND DE JOUVENEL *by Daniel Mahoney*

ANDREW NELSON LYTLE *by Mark Malvasi*

FRANCIS GRAHAM WILSON *by H. Lee Cheek*

WILL HERBERG *by Vigen Guroian*

RICHARD WEAVER *by Steven Ealy*

ERIC VOEGELIN

THE RESTORATION OF ORDER

Michael P. Federici
Mercyhurst College

ISI Books
Wilmington, Delaware
2002

The Library of Modern Thinkers is published in cooperation with Collegiate Network, Inc. Generous grants from the Sarah Scaife Foundation, Earhart Foundation, F. M. Kirby Foundation, Castle Rock Foundation, Pierre F. and Enid Goodrich Foundation, Wilbur Foundation, and the William H. Donner Foundation made this series possible. The Intercollegiate Studies Institute and Collegiate Network, Inc., gratefully acknowledge their support.

Cataloging-in-Publication Data

Federici, Michael P.

Eric Voegelin: the restoration of order / Michael P. Federici —1st ed.—Wilmington, Del. : ISI Books, 2002.

p. ; cm. (Library of modern thinkers)

ISBN 1-882926-74-9 (cloth) —ISBN 1-882926-75-7 (PBK).
1. Voegelin, Eric, 1901–1985 2. Political science—Philosophy
3. History—Philosophy 4. Philosophy, Modern—20th century
I. Title.

JA71 .F44 2002 2001097020
320.011—dc21 CIP

Published in the United States by:

ISI Books
In cooperation with Collegiate Network, Inc.
Post Office Box 4431
Wilmington, DE 19807-0431

Cover and interior design by Sam Torode

Manufactured in the United States of America

To the memory of my son,

Sayward Pierce Federici

1999–2001

CONTENTS

ACKNOWLEDGMENTS

As ONE FINISHES WRITING a book, it becomes apparent that even before the research had begun many people prepared the way. Pausing to thank such individuals and those who were instrumental in the production of the book reminds the author that writing a book is impossible outside the community of scholars, family, friends, and professionals who deserve credit for bringing the work to print.

My introduction to Eric Voegelin's work and more importantly my understanding of its power and importance as a body of scholarship occurred in several graduate courses taught by David Walsh at the Catholic University of America in the 1980s. As teacher and scholar, David was both a disciple and a critic of Voegelin's political theory. I may never have developed an interest in Voegelin without David's influence. Claes G. Ryn read and provided helpful suggestions for improving chapter 7. Always the consummate professional and model mentor, Claes's insights and encouragement shaped not only the chapter on Voegelin's critics but various parts of my analysis, including the sections dealing with conservatism and Cicero.

The University of Missouri Press has done an outstanding job publishing *The Collected Works of Eric Voegelin.* The appearance of previously unpublished materials and the insightful introductions to the new volumes were instrumental in my analysis of Voegelin's work. The publication of the *Collected Works* also made my work more difficult because I had to account for new research material and get copies of the new volumes. Jennifer Brown, publicity and exhibits manager at the University of Missouri Press, and Beverly Jarrett, director and editor in chief at that press, made sure that I had the necessary volumes in a timely manner. Their assistance is greatly appreciated.

Eric Wagner read an early version of the manuscript and provided helpful suggestions that improved the clarity of my writing and analysis. Greg Butler at New Mexico State University, Jeff Polet at Malone College, and Richard Gamble at Palm Beach Atlantic College were all part of a small group of scholars that provided encouragement and served as sounding boards for my ideas.

Jeff Nelson, publisher of ISI Books, approached me at a conference in Williamsburg, Virginia, in the summer of 1998 about writing the book. I am grateful for his confidence in my work and oversight of the project. Jeremy Beer has been a diligent and professional editor. The vast improvements from the original manuscript to the final product are due largely to his constant efforts to sharpen the writing, analysis, and focus of the book. There are many individuals in the ISI community whom I'm thankful to have worked with on this project and others. Gary Gregg, Mark Henrie, Paul Rhein, Mike Wallacavage, Winfield J. C. Myers, and Jason Duke all have contributed to this project.

Parts of chapter 4 first appeared in an article published in the *Intercollegiate Review* as "Logophobia." Parts of chapter 7 appeared in "Voegelin's Christian Critics" in *Modern Age.* I appreciate the Intercollegiate Studies Institute's permission to use parts of these articles.

My colleagues in the political science department at Mercyhurst College, Randy Clemons and Brian Ripley, supported me during the writing of this book. Their professionalism and collegiality provided me with a working environment conducive to researching and writing a book. Dr. William P. Garvey, president of Mercyhurst College, supported my work by granting me a sabbatical leave for the spring 2001 term. The release from teaching responsibilities was vital to the completion of this volume.

Finally, I would like to thank my family. In the four years

that I worked on this book two of my three children were born and one died. My son Sayward Pierce, to whom the book is dedicated, gave me inspiration. He was a source of strength from the moment of his birth, when it seemed impossible that he would survive, through the struggles of his short life to his death at eighteen months of age. He was never able to voice his thoughts or desires; he never saw light or beauty; he never heard the joyous sounds of life; he never smiled to thank the many people who cared for him during his difficult struggle. But somehow the boy who lived his life in a coma, unable to communicate with the world around him, was the source of innumerable acts of kindness and love. His life and his memory provided his daddy with the determination to write this book. His two sisters, Elizabeth and Amy Rebecca, have filled my life with joy, without which professional accomplishments seem meaningless. His mom, my loving wife Frances, has endured the burden of my frustrations while writing this book. Her support and encouragement kept me focused on my work and her love reminded me why I work.

ABBREVIATIONS

A	*Anamnesis*, translated and edited by Gerhart Niemeyer (Notre Dame, Ind.: University of Notre Dame Press, 1978).
AS	*The Authoritarian State: An Essay on the Problem of the Austrian State*, translated by Ruth Hein, edited with an introduction by Gilbert Weiss, historical commentary by Erika Weinzierl (Columbia, Mo.: University of Missouri Press, 1999). Originally published in 1936 as *Der autoritäre Staat: Ein Versuch über das österreichische Staatsproblem*.
AR	*Autobiographical Reflections*, edited with an introduction by Ellis Sandoz (Baton Rouge, La.: Louisiana State University Press, 1989).
CEV	*Conversations with Eric Voegelin*, edited with an

introduction by R. Eric O'Connor (Montreal: Thomas More Institute, 1980).

FER — *From Enlightenment to Revolution*, edited by John H. Hallowell (Durham, N.C.: Duke University Press, 1975).

HG — *Hitler and the Germans*, translated, edited, and with an introduction by Detlev Clemens and Brendan Purcell (Columbia, Mo.: University of Missouri Press, 1999). Lectures delivered in the summer of 1964 at the University of Munich.

HPI I — *History of Political Ideas, vol. I: Hellenism, Rome, and Early Christianity*, edited with an introduction by Athanasios Moulakis (Columbia, Mo.: University of Missouri Press, 1997).

HPI II — *History of Political Ideas, vol. II: The Middle Ages to Aquinas*, edited with an introduction by Peter von Sivers (Columbia, Mo.: University of Missouri Press, 1997).

HPI III — *History of Political Ideas, vol. III: The Later Middle Ages*, edited with an introduction by David Walsh (Columbia, Mo.: University of Missouri Press, 1998).

HPI IV — *History of Political Ideas, vol. IV: Renaissance and Reformation*, edited with an introduction by David L. Morse and William M. Thompson

(Columbia, Mo.: University of Missouri Press, 1998).

HPI V — *History of Political Ideas, vol. V: Religion and the Rise of Modernity*, edited with an introduction by James L. Wiser (Columbia, Mo.: University of Missouri Press, 1998).

HPI VI — *History of Political Ideas, vol. VI: Revolution and the New Science*, edited with an introduction by Barry Cooper (Columbia, Mo.: University of Missouri Press, 1998).

HPI VII — *History of Political Ideas, vol. VII: The New Order and Last Orientation*, edited with an introduction by Jürgen Gebhardt and Thomas A. Hollweck (Columbia, Mo.: University of Missouri Press, 1999).

HPI VIII — *History of Political Ideas, vol. VIII: Crisis and the Apocalypse of Man*, edited with an introduction by David Walsh (Columbia, Mo.: University of Missouri Press, 1999).

HRI — *The History of the Race Idea*, translated by Ruth Hein, edited with an introduction by Klaus Vondung (Columbia, Mo.: University of Missouri Press, 1998). Originally published in 1933 as *Die Rassenidee in der Geistesgeschichte.*

NSP — *The New Science of Politics*, foreword by Dante

	Germino (Chicago: The University of Chicago Press, 1952). Reprinted in 1983 and 1987 by Midway.
OFAM	*On the Form of the American Mind*, translated by Ruth Hein, edited with an introduction by Jürgen Gebhardt and Barry Cooper (Baton Rouge, La.: Louisiana State University Press, 1995). Originally published in 1928 as *Über die Form des amerikanischen Geistes.*
OH I	*Order and History, vol. I: Israel and Revelation*, edited with an introduction by Maurice P. Hogan (Columbia, Mo.: University of Missouri Press, 2001). Originally published in 1956 by Louisiana State University Press.
OH II	*Order and History, vol. II: The World of the Polis*, edited with an introduction by Athanasios Moulakis (Columbia, Mo.: University of Missouri Press, 2000). Originally published in 1957 by Louisiana State University Press.
OH III	*Order and History, vol. III: Plato and Aristotle*, edited with an introduction by Dante Germino (Columbia, Mo.: University of Missouri Press, 2000). Originally published in 1957 by Louisiana State University Press.
OH IV	*Order and History, vol. IV: The Ecumenic Age*,

edited with an introduction by Michael Franz (Columbia, Mo.: University of Missouri Press, 2000). Originally published in 1974 by Louisiana State University Press.

OH V — *Order and History, vol. V: In Search of Order*, edited with an introduction by Ellis Sandoz (Columbia, Mo.: University of Missouri Press, 2000). Originally published in 1987 by Louisiana State University Press.

PE 1953–1965 — *Published Essays 1953–1965*, edited with an introduction by Ellis Sandoz (Columbia, Mo.: University of Missouri Press, 2000).

PE 1966–1985 — *Published Essays 1966–1985*, edited with an introduction by Ellis Sandoz (Baton Rouge, La.: Louisiana State University Press, 1990).

PR — *The Political Religions*, translated by Virginia Ann Schildhauer, edited with an introduction by Manfred Henningsen (Columbia, Mo.: University of Missouri Press, 2000). Originally published in 1938 as *Die politischen Religionen*.

RS — *Race and State*, translated by Ruth Hein, edited with an introduction by Klaus Vondung (Columbia, Mo.: University of Missouri Press, 1997). Originally published in 1933 as *Rasse und Staat*.

SPG	*Science, Politics and Gnosticism* (Chicago: Regnery Gateway, 1968).
WIH	*What Is History? And Other Late Unpublished Writings*, edited with an introduction by Thomas A. Hollweck and Paul Caringella (Baton Rouge, La.: Louisiana State University Press, 1990).

INTRODUCTION

WRITING A BOOK about Eric Voegelin's political theory is a challenging task. The author must explain the philosophical and historical substance of Voegelin's work, capture the importance of his contribution to scholarship and to the restoration of Western civilization, and evaluate criticisms of his political theory. Several factors, including the volume of his scholarship, make forming these objectives into a cogent study of his political philosophy a formidable project. Voegelin wrote twenty-one books and more than one hundred scholarly articles that together mark the intellectual and existential journey of a seminal twentieth-century philosopher.[1] The philosophical density and historical scope of his work add to the challenge of explaining and analyzing his political theory. Moreover, there are several dimensions to Voegelin's intellectual achievement, including a history of political ideas, a new science of politics, a philosophy of order and history, and a philosophy of consciousness.

The volume, scope, theoretical complexity, and multidimensionality of his work make it difficult to convey the meaning of his political philosophy intricately and to connect all its aspects in a brief book. To review as much of Voegelin's political theory as possible, and to introduce it to a wide audience, it is necessary to be expository when discussing some parts of his work and analytical when discussing others. This book focuses on the central components of Voegelin's political philosophy and tries to leave esoteric issues regarding his work to more specialized scholars.

Whatever the level of analysis, explaining Voegelin's political philosophy requires both the exposition of his ideas and an understanding of the context in which they were created. The context for Voegelin's political philosophy includes the political and historical circumstances in which he wrote and the evolution of his scholarly work as a whole, with its shifts in emphasis and its development of new philosophical vistas. It is also important to have some grasp of Voegelin's biographical profile, since his political philosophy was shaped by personal encounters he had with totalitarianism and other spiritually suffocating ideologies.

But as complex as Voegelin's political philosophy may seem, there is a common thread running through his work. Whether

Voegelin was focusing on the philosophy of history and order, the philosophy of consciousness, the race problem in Germany, or the history of political ideas, his primary concern was to engage in the open philosophical search for the truth of existence. The responsibility of political philosophers who make this search their lifework is to articulate the truth of existence and defend it from untruth. The search for truth and order is always met with resistance—not only in society but in the imagination of the philosopher who searches for ways to articulate truth by sifting through alternative conceptions of reality (*OH V*, 53–54). The search cannot take place outside the war in the imagination between competing perceptions of reality. The presence of untruth is a part of the structure of consciousness that must be confronted and overcome. Voegelin's search for the truth of existence included resisting prevalent ideological distortions, diagnosing their spiritual causes, and tracing their historical development. This approach put Voegelin at odds with the dominant forces of his age.

The Contemporary Context

Our own intellectual and cultural context adds to the difficulty of explaining Voegelin's political philosophy. Voegelin's work is not well known outside a relatively small group of academics and their students. Yet within this domain Voegelin's influence is impressive. His work has inspired a growing secondary literature and his political philosophy has been applied to a variety of topics in a broad range of academic fields. His philosophy of history and philosophy of consciousness have influenced the work of thinkers who are significant in their own right. Among these are Gerhart Niemeyer, Flannery O'Connor, David Walsh, Marion Montgomery, Russell Kirk, James L. Wiser, Ellis Sandoz, Dante Germino, and Jürgen Gebhardt. Further evidence of Voegelin's influence is the creation in 1987 of the Voegelin Institute at Louisiana State University and the establishment of the Centre for Voegelin Studies in the Department of Religions and Theology at the University of Manchester. But while Voegelin's work has influenced several first-rate scholars, his political theory has not found its way into the broader culture.

Several factors have contributed to the obscurity of Voegelin's work.[2] For one thing, as Ellis Sandoz notes, Voegelin made few concessions to those readers who were not prepared to intellectually digest difficult historical and philosophical material. While Voegelin did write some essays intended to be accessible to a wider audience, until recently many of these works were either unpublished or only available in German. In addition, the recent secondary literature on Voegelin tends to focus on his deeper theoretical work. Another factor that contributes to Voegelin's obscurity is that while he lectured at some of the leading universities in America and Europe, he spent a good part of his academic career at Louisiana State University, a school that did not provide Voegelin with institutional prestige. Furthermore, because Voegelin was so intent on working his way through a broad range of historical and philosophical sources, he generally did not take on Ph.D. students.[3] Consequently, he has not benefited from the activity of dozens of graduate students passing on his ideas to new generations of scholars. Finally, Voegelin was often misunderstood or ignored because his political philosophy was intellectually alien to conventional ideological dispositions. Not only did the *New York Times* fail to review even one of Voegelin's books while he was living;[4] its obituary of Voegelin conveys no sense of his contribution to scholarship, his intellectual genius, or his imaginative vision.[5]

Time did publish a feature five-page article on Voegelin's analysis of gnosticism, which appeared about a year after the publication of *The New Science of Politics*. The context for the article is interesting, and it provides some sense of how Voegelin's work was perceived by the broader culture in a rare case of its popular dissemination. In the March 9, 1953, issue of *Time*, which celebrated the magazine's thirtieth year of publication, the editors put forth a list of "convictions" and a "birthday thesis" based largely—and remarkably—on Voegelin's analysis of gnosticism.[6] The portion of the article that dealt with Voegelin's work was a rough sketch of his understanding of gnosticism and how it has influenced the evolution of Western thinking and politics. The title of the article, "Journalism and Joachim's Children," was a reference to the thirteenth-century Calabrisan monk Joachim of Fiore (Flora), who figures prominently in Voegelin's analysis of the Western cultural crisis.[7]

The response to the article was, as one might expect, varied. In the following two issues, *Time* ran several related letters to the editor. Some were comical: "I find your recent gobbledygook about Gnosticism revolting. You and the Pope can play God if you want to, but whether or not man can ultimately attain perfection is far beyond the depth of either of you, let alone anything to do with newsreporting. . . ."[8] Other readers applauded *Time*. One reader thanked the editors for the "absorbing synopsis of Political Scientist Voegelin's thesis." Another called the article "[t]he most realistic and mature analysis of the world situation to appear in a leading magazine."[9] But, in general, if the almost three dozen letters to the editor were any indication of the general public's ability to understand Voegelin's work, it seems probable that popular news magazines were not the best outlet for disseminating Voegelin's political philosophy.

Further evidence of the problems one faces when explaining Voegelin's political theory is the fact that he was classified by critics and supporters alike as belonging to one or another of a broad spectrum of categories.[10] He refused, however, to identify himself with ideological labels,[11] and therefore there is no ready-made ideological group prepared to embrace his political theory. His political philosophy tends to attract individuals who are more contemplative than they are political, and just where Voegelin's political philosophy fits in contemporary political categories is not clear. Even today, while his followers tend to be politically and intellectually conservative,[12] they include individuals with a broad range of political intuitions. This may be attributed, in part, to Voegelin's insistence on an open philosophical search and his rejection of political ideology. But it can also be attributed to an often lamentably high degree of abstractness in his political theory.

Chapter 1 will give readers some indication of who Voegelin was and will explain the context of his scholarly work. Later chapters emphasize Voegelin's political philosophy. It may be that this emphasis on his political writings will leave some readers with the impression that Voegelin's work on the philosophy of consciousness is less important, or that there is a lack of continuity between his political philosophy and his philosophy of consciousness. To a certain extent this implication is intentional. Voegelin's work on the philosophy of consciousness is, no doubt, a genuine achievement, and in some respects it represents a natural evolution and culmination of his work. Voegelin believed that the crisis of the West demanded a transformation of consciousness. Yet there is an extent to which his philosophy of consciousness is distant from politics, and, unlike most of his earlier work, it has less direct relevance to political life. Furthermore, Voegelin's work on the philosophy of consciousness is highly abstract and philosophically dense—it is difficult to imagine a philosophy of consciousness being otherwise. Thus, for most beginning students of Voegelin's work, his philosophy of consciousness is not the place to start. Voegelin's political writings serve as the best introduction to his political theory. Before going on to explain and examine that theory in detail, it is worth introducing the major components of Voegelin's thought.

The Restoration of Engendering Experience

Faced with widespread and profound cultural, social, and moral decay, Voegelin theorized that the West had lost its consciousness of certain historical experiences vital to the formation of political, social, and existential order.[13] In Voegelin's terms, historical experiences and their corresponding language symbols illuminated the truth of reality. Language was necessary to articulate "experiences of order" and preserve them over time, since such experiences were rare. The truth of existence embodied in experience was an ordering force because it attuned the open soul to the Agathon (the Good). And a just political and social order, like the just soul, is dependent on this sort of attunement. Unfortunately, historical experience cannot have an ordering effect if the language symbols that preserve it lose their original meaning, as occurs when they are transformed or obscured by ideological movements. Such movements act to detach language symbols from their engendering experiences. To regain consciousness of the engendering experiences—and in turn to restore social, political, and existential order—the philosopher must "reactivate the engendering experience in his psyche" and "recapture the truth of reality living in the symbols."[14] In particular, the language symbols of myth, revelation, history, and especially philosophy must be restored to luminosity—that is, reattached to the historical experiences that they attempt to convey—before rational discussion of the questions of order can occur. This recovery of meaning requires the philosopher to recreate the experience imaginatively in an act of meditation and to create "reflective symbols" that articulate the truth of the "original symbols." This understanding of the modern crisis as a loss of consciousness of symbols and experience helps to explain why Voegelin turned to the philosophy of consciousness in his later work.[15]

Contemporary usage of the word "philosophy" illustrates the consequences of detaching language symbols from their engendering experiences. "Philosophy" has become, in common usage, to mean the same as "ideology" or "value system." But philosophical clarity depends on distinctions such as that between philosophy and knowledge (*episteme*) on the one hand and ideology and opinion (*doxa*) on the other. The contemporary use of philosophy and ideology as synonyms implies, for instance, that the philosophies of Plato and Aristotle should not be regarded as truth-claims about reality, but simply as two ideologies among many that individuals are free to choose based on their personal preferences or political interests. The political implications of the symbol "philosophy" becoming opaque are evident in the emergence of "spin doctors," a character type that Plato classified as *philodoxers* (lovers of appearance and opinion). Their intentional distortion of reality erodes the ability of individuals to see life for what it is. Modern *philodoxers* draw their arguments from the common misconceptions of the day. In such an environment politics is not a search for either truth or the foundation of order based on that truth. Politics is rather a power game played by *philodoxers* who sell their opinions with the Sophistic understanding that what matters is merely power, not truth. This context makes it difficult to establish the existence of truth (*aletheia*) about reality, particularly transcendent reality. Indeed, references to an objective reality are now usually met with deep existential and intellectual skepticism, if not complete intolerance. Voegelin classifies this reaction to philosophical insight as "narcissistic closure." He believes that it is characteristic of the spiritual alienation and estrangement of modern man (*PE 1966–1985*, 1–35). Meaningful discussion cannot take place under such circumstances because the preconditions for rational debate do not exist (*PE 1966–1985*, 36–51).[16]

Because important language symbols have lost their meaning, Voegelin found it not only necessary to restore the original meaning of old symbols, but also to create new terms to explain philosophical issues. Examples of Voegelin's new symbols are "logophobia" (fear and hatred of philosophy) and "pseudological speculation" (nontheoretical speculation—speculation that is closed to aspects of reality because of adherence to rigid ideological preconceptions such as that seen in "spiritually diseased" thinkers like Karl Marx).[17] Voegelin created these terms to explain the spiritual depravity that engenders ideological systems. The creation of new terms and concepts was a necessary part of creating or restoring a new science of politics, the science of classical political philosophy, which was able to effectively analyze and diagnose the modern crisis.[18] The combination of unfamiliar philosophical terms and neologisms opened Voegelin to the charge of being pedantic or esoteric. But he was neither. Upon careful study of Voegelin's political theory, it becomes clear that the use of unfamiliar philosophical terms and neologisms was warranted by the nature and context of his political philosophy. Penetrating to experiential meaning and the truth of reality in an age of deforming ideologies required the reactivation of the meaning of symbols that articulated the experiences of reality, and the creation of new ones to describe complex philosophical problems. Voegelin was not being intellectually vain in his terminology; he was attempting to genuinely describe reality and to restore political science.[19]

Rejection of Dogma and Doctrine

Although Voegelin recognized the practical need for doctrine and dogma, he was philosophically opposed to the codification of the good as dogma, doctrine, or "ism." For Voegelin, the philosophical objective was to get beyond traditions and codifications of reality to the "predogmatic reality of knowledge" (*A*, 189), by which he meant the engendering experiences with reality that revealed the truth of the human condition. The problem was that experiences and symbols are apt to diverge when original experiences are formulated into doctrines. That is, the process of doctrinalization shifts the focus of human consciousness from experience to dogma. The separation of doctrine and experience is problematic because dogmatism and doctrinalization prohibit philosophical searching, since such searching is seen as infidelity to established principles.

Given this understanding of engendering experience and its relationship to language symbols, it is not surprising that Voegelin was so adamant in opposing doctrinalization. In fact, it has been suggested that one of the central components of his philosophy is not merely antidoctrinalization but dedoctrinalization.[20] But although doctrinalization is an obstacle to the recovery of experience, how can the engendering experiences of reality be maintained as a living force without some degree of codification? Voegelin's answer will be discussed in chapter 7. Most people are incapable of the meditative exercise that Voegelin believed necessary to imaginatively re-create such engendering experiences. So how can they participate in the good without recourse to doctrine? Voegelin was acutely aware that human beings were prone to fall from the truth of order and that it had to be regained repeatedly. Yet it is illuminating that although Voegelin recognized this fact he nonetheless stridently opposed doctrinalization in the work of philosophy.[21]

Voegelin's New Science of Politics

Diagnosing the Western crisis requires the creation of a philosophical framework that can identify the sources of disorder and penetrate to their spiritual causes. This effort gave rise to Voegelin's "new" science of politics. His approach was new in the sense that it was a radical break from the dominant ideologically driven methodologies of his day. Yet it was old in the sense that Voegelin's conception of science was a return to the classical approach of Plato and Aristotle. This reconstituted approach to scientific analysis was necessary because of the existing state of scholarship in the twentieth century.[22] Ideologies like positivism place methodological demands on scholars that make it impossible to accurately diagnose the ills of the Western world. These ideologies are inadequate because they are philosophically closed to the complete scope of reality—that is, their methods and presuppositions prohibit theoretical analysis of questions regarding transcendent reality. Ideologies are obstacles to scientific and scholarly analysis of the modern crisis and indeed are part of the crisis itself.

Reawakening Western consciousness to the experiences of order that are the very substance of civilization demands an open and complete search for the divine source of order. This process of remembrance (*anamnesis*) suggests that the truth of experiential reality has not been lost forever but rather lies dormant in the Western mind, waiting to be imaginatively aroused by a spiritually sensitive soul. Voegelin's philosophical framework attempted to break down the ideological barriers to the search for order and the recovery of transcendent consciousness, which is why he devoted a significant portion of his scholarship to the problems of ideology and methodology. It is also why he rejected doctrines of order (as opposed to the philosophy of order) and why he devoted so much of his effort to the openness of the search (*zetema*). Voegelin's political philosophy illuminated a path; it embodied the spirit in which the search for the transcendent source of order should be conducted; it did not create an ideological system, political program, or social doctrine.[23] The primary objective of this political philosophy was not to recover historical information but to recover an understanding of the process by which man becomes conscious of transcendent-divine reality.

Voegelin and Christianity

One of the most intensely debated areas of Voegelin's work, especially within the political Right, is his analysis of Christianity. Voegelin is criticized from the Right for his treatment of Christian doctrine and his apparent depreciation of Christianity in *The Ecumenic Age*. It is thought by some that he did not sufficiently embrace Christian faith, including the divinity of Christ and the Resurrection.[24] Furthermore, Voegelin placed a significant part of the blame for the modern crisis—particularly its gnostic character—at the feet of Christianity. His analysis of thinkers who contributed to the Western crisis included St. Paul, St. Francis of Assisi, and St. John the Evangelist. Their "eschatological pathos" (*NSP*, 108) provided the spiritual impetus for millenarianism and other immanentizing aspects of modern ideologies. Voegelin's Christian critics, in short, charge that he portrays Christianity as more a cause of than a cure for the modern crisis.

Framework for Studying Voegelin's Work

The historical range, volume, and philosophical complexity of Voegelin's ideas require the author who is charged with explaining and analyzing his work to weave together a series of threads in his thought that span roughly sixty years of a prodigiously productive career. The different aspects of Voegelin's thought can be better analyzed if Voegelin's major works are divided into four parts: (1) early works; (2) *History of Political Ideas*; (3) *The New Science of Politics*; *Science, Politics and Gnosticism*; and the first three volumes of *Order and History*; and (4) the final two volumes of *Order and History*. This framework makes it easier to identify and explain the two significant shifts or developments in his work that came when he broke with his *History of Political Ideas* project and when he revised the framework for *Order and History* after volume three. If carefully examined, the changes in the direction of Voegelin's work are evidence of his philosophical quest for truth. Looking back from the end to the beginning of his philosophical quest, it is apparent that his commitment to philosophical inquiry (*zetema*) is so ardent that his search is directed by the pull (*helkein*) of truth (*aletheia*) rather than by the desire to create a closed ideological system for political and social action. The consequence of Voegelin's philosophical searching is that the direction and path of his work is not straight and narrow. There is a central direction, a focus, to his quest, but retracing his philosophical steps creates a kaleidoscopic view of his search for order. Depending on what part of the journey is examined, the picture provides different, but not incongruous, perspectives.

Readers who are more experienced students of Voegelin will find something of interest in this book. In chapter 7, for example, Voegelin's critics are addressed in a way that should provoke discussion and debate among those who share his desire to ground political science in transcendent reality. Yet the focus of this volume is to disseminate Voegelin's political theory to a broader audience than seems to have been reached by the existing literature. This book will be one of the first to provide a basic introduction to Voegelin's political theory; its intention is to encourage the study of Voegelin's work by providing an outline of his political philosophy. If the book leads the reader to further explore Voegelin's books and articles, then it will have accomplished its main objective. Given the reputation that his work has as intellectually intimidating, if not impenetrable, a book of this kind is justified as a way of facilitating the study of Voegelin, especially at the undergraduate level. But no scholarly work, however well written, will substitute for reading primary texts. Nor will an introductory book eliminate the frustration and difficulty that often accompany the study of Voegelin's works. Deep and philosophically penetrating works require an investment of mind and soul that is bound to be as challenging as it is rewarding; there are no shortcuts. Part of the value of great philosophical thinkers is the struggle one must undertake to re-live their intellectual and existential journey imaginatively. Appreciating Voegelin's work requires one to replicate his existential journey to some degree. What took Voegelin a lifetime to understand and explain cannot be known in a brief period of time or by reading one monograph about his political theory. But the investment of time and intellectual energy is well worth the effort. The reward for studying Voegelin is a greater understanding of the Western crisis and an encounter with a prescription for restoration that is among the most philosophically penetrating in modern and postmodern times. Voegelin's historical, political, and philosophical insights provide the reader with a level of theoretical understanding that can be used to make sense of a historical period that cries out for explanation. Moreover, a necessary stop on the road to postmodernity is some understanding of what modernity is and what it means in the larger historical and philosophical context. Getting beyond modernity requires that the ideological deformations of the modern period be purged from the soul and consciousness of Western man. On this score, Voegelin has few rivals.

CHAPTER ONE

BIOGRAPHICAL SKETCH AND EARLY WORKS

VOEGELIN WAS BORN in Cologne, Germany, on January 3, 1901. His family moved to Vienna when he was nine. While a resident of Austria, he attended the University of Vienna, where he completed his doctorate in political science in 1922.[1] He wrote his Ph.D. dissertation on "Reciprocal Influence and Doubling" (*Wechselwirkung und Gezweiung*), drawing on the sociological work of Georg Simmel and Othmar Spann.[2] During his doctoral studies he attended seminars by Ludwig von Mises and developed a lasting friendship with F. A. Hayek, among other students.[3] After finishing his doctorate, he studied German constitutional law in Berlin and Heidelberg before becoming an assistant at the University of Vienna to his mentor Hans Kelsen, the author of the Austrian Constitution of 1920 (*OFAM*, xxxvi). Voegelin studied for a summer at Oxford, where he attended lectures by the classicist Gilbert Murray. From 1924 to 1926 he studied at Columbia, Harvard, and Wisconsin.[4] He attended lectures by John Dewey, Alfred North Whitehead, Irwin Edman, and John R. Commons, among others, and he was also introduced to Scottish Common Sense philosophy, the American and British intellectual tradition, and the works of George Santayana. These influences contributed to Voegelin's intellectual evolution.[5] He explains, "It was during this time that I got the first inkling of what the continued tradition of Classic philosophy on the common sense level, without necessarily the technical apparatus of an Aristotle, could mean for the intellectual climate and the cohesion of a society" (*AR*, 29). This common sense tradition was noticeably absent from the "German social scene" and not very influential in France. His American studies inspired his first book, *On the Form of the American Mind* (*Über die Form des amerikanischen Geistes*), published in 1928, in which he devotes separate chapters to Santayana and Commons.

Voegelin's American experience was intellectually formative, sparking a significant transformation in his thought. When he came to America in 1924 he was what Gilbert Weiss describes as a "hermeneutic sociologist in the tradition of Max Weber." But while studying in the U.S., Voegelin was deeply influenced by American pragmatism and the tradition of common sense philosophy. As Weiss explains, "When he returned home from the United States, he felt considerably freer of the neo-Kantian limitations of Weber's thinking as well as of the abstract discourses of the German-speaking intellectual world in general . . ." (*AS*, 7). Neo-Kantian methodology—advocated by Hans Kelsen and others under whom Voegelin studied—was prevalent in the Viennese intellectual environment. But Voegelin came to recognize that Kelsen's theory of law was flawed.[6] It reduced political theory to a theory of law and in particular to the logic of legal norms. This approach to political theory left out what Voegelin came to understand was essential to political science—experience with transcendent reality and its symbolic expression. Voegelin's rejection of neo-Kantianism is explicit in *The Authoritarian State* (1936), but already in *On the Form of the American Mind* Voegelin germinates a classical and Christian approach to political philosophy as well as concepts like "intellectual formation" that provide the substance of his understanding of self-interpretation and representation as discussed, for example, in *The New Science of Politics*. The language symbols used to articulate the meaning of life in a society are part of the self-reflective process that reveals the experiential substance of a political unit. The symbols of self-interpretation illuminate social and political reality and they provide an interpretation of reality that the political philosopher can measure against his theoretical understanding. But the neo-Kantian approach was a variant of positivism that closed off certain areas of human experience to scientific investigation. Voegelin realized that to penetrate to the core problems of political order it was necessary to "reconstruct the full range of political science" rather than to limit scientific analysis to arbitrary methodological constraints (*AR*, 22). Voegelin's rejection of neo-Kantian methodology and his movement toward experientially based philosophy marks an early stage in the development of his new science of politics. As a result of his American experience, Voegelin began to reject modern epistemology and to embrace the classical and Christian tradition that would shape his work for the remainder of his life.[7] As Weiss states, for Voegelin, "reality was no more an external object determined by the *a priori* structure of a neo-Kantian subject of cognition but a process *in* which man participates in a variety of ways" (*AS*, 8).

After his trip to the U.S., Voegelin studied at the Sorbonne, where he focused on French literature and philosophy. He returned to Austria in 1927 and became interested in political developments there. His intellectual and personal life, in these years, was affected by the increasing influence of National Socialism. The civil war (February 1934) and clash of political ideologies led Voegelin to explore the problems of radical ideologies. In 1933 he published two books on the race question,[8] *Race and State* (*Rasse und Staat*) and *The History of the Race Idea* (*Die Rassenidee in der Geistesgeschichte*). *The History of the Race Idea*, was withdrawn from circulation by the Nazis and the remaining copies destroyed. His work on contemporary Austrian politics and ideology was published in 1936 as *The Authoritarian State* (*Die Authoritäre Staat*). It too was withdrawn from circulation by the Nazis in 1938.

His published works and reputation made him a political target for the Nazis. After the *Anschluss*, Voegelin was fired from his academic position at the University of Vienna and he began to plan his emigration. He was investigated by the Gestapo but avoided arrest. In 1938, shortly after Hitler's invasion of Austria, he fled Austria and made his way to the United States via Switzerland.[9] At about the time of his emigration, Voegelin had completed *The Political Religions* (*Die politischen Religionen*), which was due to be published in April 1938, one month after the Nazi annexation of Austria. The National Socialist occupation of Austria, however, resulted in the confiscation of the book and printing ceased. It was republished in 1939 by Bermann-Fisher and issued in Stockholm.

Voegelin wrote a new preface to *The Political Religions* for the Bermann-Fisher edition that responded to Thomas Mann's charge that he was not sufficiently critical of the Nazis.[10] In the new preface Voegelin emphasized his opposition to collectivism and stated the importance of carefully analyzing the spiritual and religious roots of totalitarianism rather than providing a moral condemnation of such movements. Voegelin did not believe that engaging in "ethical counter-propaganda" was the best approach to confronting National Socialism. He argued that focusing on ethical condemnation obscured the nature of the problem because it "diverts attention from the fact that a deeper and much more dangerous evil is hidden behind the ethically condemnable actions." The danger, Voegelin felt, was that ethical condemnation alone leaves the impression that breaking the conventional moral code is the crux of the evil. The depth of the anticollectivist argument and resistance to movements like National Socialism must run deeper. Resistance must penetrate to the religious roots of morally abhorrent actions and ideas, which provide a much more philosophically and spiritually sound foundation for opposition than attacking the problem at the level of moral convention: "Resistance against a satanical substance that is not only morally but also religiously evil can only be derived from an equally strong, religiously good force. One cannot fight a satanical force with morality and humanity alone." Voegelin also objected to the argument that National Socialism represented a return to the "Dark Ages." Such a view suggested that the enlightened ideas of modernity provided protection from collectivism. Yet Voegelin pointed out that the religious core of the modern spirit, humanitarianism, contributed to the rise of National Socialism. He explained that "the doctrine of humanitarianism is the soil in which such anti-Christian religious movements as National Socialism were able to prosper" (*PR*, 24). Resistance to collectivist movements like National Socialism was conducted by individuals who seemed unaware that they were intellectually and spiritually infected with the same pseudo-spiritual secularism that shaped the political movements they were opposing. Voegelin realized that efficacious resistance required the restoration of genuine spirituality. Ironically, the effort to restore genuine spirituality was met with resistance on the grounds that such an effort was, like National Socialism, a return to the "Dark Ages."

The problem of National Socialism was indicative of the larger Western crisis and Voegelin's response to it was already evident in *The Political Religions*. The problem was "the secularization of the soul" and the separation of the secular soul from "its roots in religiousness." Recovery was only possible through "religious renewal" and it could "only be initiated by great religious personalities" (*PR*, 24). The starting point for analyzing the crisis was to explain the "non-Christian, non-national intellectual and mass movements into which the Europe of Christian nation-states was in the process of breaking up" (*SPG*, 5). The identification of these movements and the explanation of their pseudo-spiritual characteristics constituted the beginning of Voegelin's classification of modern political movements as political religions. This insight led to the development of what he would later call "gnosticism," a defining characteristic of modernity.

Voegelin's first five books and his early work generally are shaped by contemporary European political events and developments. Sandoz explained that "the gist of Voegelin's effort, the grit around which he created his pearl, arose because of his own personal, intellectual, and spiritual resistance to the Nazi horror experienced as a profound affront to his humanity, one endangering mankind itself and identified more broadly as the crisis of modernity."[11] The experience with totalitarianism made Voegelin, like other European exiles (e.g., Aleksandr Solzhenitsyn, F. A. Hayek), sensitive to the problems of state authority and individual freedom. His view of democratic politics was colored by this sensitivity. The rise of the welfare state in the West, for example, was cause for caution because of the parallel structure and ideological commonality between liberalism and totalitarianism.[12] Due to this personal and political context, Voegelin's early works tended to deal with politics in an explicit manner and tended to lack the degree of philosophical abstractness notable in his later work. They also lacked the philosophical depth of his more mature work. Aspects of his later thought could be identified in them, but the differences were significant enough to consider them as constituting a separate phase of his career.

Voegelin spent from 1938 to 1958 in the United States. During this period he wrote the *History of Political Ideas* volumes, *The New Science of Politics*, and the first three volumes of *Order and History*, among other scholarly works. He became an American citizen in 1944 and taught for sixteen years at Louisiana State University after brief stays at Harvard, Bennington

College, and the University of Alabama. He moved to Munich in 1958 after accepting a position at the University of Munich as professor and director of the Institute for Political Science. His inaugural Munich lecture was published as *Science, Politics and Gnosticism*. According to Sandoz, one of the reasons that Voegelin returned to Germany was because he wanted to establish an institute in Munich that would help bring American constitutional democracy to Germany.[13]

In 1964 Voegelin gave a series of lectures on Hitler and the rise of the Nazis.[14] These lectures explained Hitler's rise to power, the circumstances in which he rose to power, and the effects of the Nazi experience on postwar Germany and German national identity. Voegelin's lectures on Hitler and the Germans are a good illustration of how Voegelin aimed in his work to diagnose and provide a prescriptive response to problems of disorder. Moreover, the Nazi lectures demonstrate how, at least for works like this, Voegelin's political philosophy was not detached from politics but directed at the core questions of contemporary political order. For Voegelin, National Socialism was a concrete case of a gnostic ideology that had gained a foothold in a democratic society. It illustrated the politically and socially destructive capacity of gnosticism and the Western crisis in its advanced stages.[15]

Voegelin's most valuable contribution to our understanding of the Nazi problem was his analysis of its spiritual dimension. The rise of the Nazis and the commission of unthinkable horrors were not the result of one spiritually deranged man or even a spiritually deranged elite class. It was necessary for the better part of German society to participate in the Nazi rise to power and Nazi atrocities for them to occur. But, Voegelin argued, the Allies' attempt at denazification had failed; guilt for Nazism had been placed by the German people only on the elite. As a result, Voegelin suggested, the spiritual disease that caused the Nazi problem was still present in postwar Germany. This conclusion, formulated twenty years after the end of the war, was not well received in the German press or by some of Voegelin's colleagues at the University of Munich, and Voegelin began to receive personal threats (*HG*, 1). These experiences and the general ideological climate in Germany discouraged his efforts to make the American experience of constitutional democracy a living force in Germany.

Consequently, Voegelin returned to the U.S. in 1969 to a position at Stanford University's Hoover Institution on War, Revolution and Peace. He held the position of Henry Salvatori Distinguished Scholar until 1974, the same year that the fourth volume of *Order and History* (*The Ecumenic Age*) was published. While holding no formal academic post after 1974, Voegelin continued to work diligently on the final volume of *Order and History* (*In Search of Order*) and other projects.[16] Including the *History of Political Ideas* volumes, Voegelin wrote twenty-one books and over one hundred articles. He died on January 19, 1985.

Voegelin has been described as "a gentleman thinker." While he held to the highest standards of scholarship he avoided pedantry. He was also a man of deep philosophical learning who did not dilute his discussion of scholarly matters to please his audience. He was uninterested in small talk and made efficient use of his time, and he did not hesitate to challenge conventional ideas and clichés that he believed distorted the truth. But he did make at least one exception—on the occasion of his naturalization as an American citizen. Voegelin had been given a handbook to study for his naturalization interview that contained false information. He asked his friend Robert Heilman, "If the answers in the handbook are wrong, should I give the right answers or say what the handbook says?" Heilman advised the latter and Voegelin passed his exam easily. Voegelin was devoted to his work and rarely if ever watched television. He read the *New York Times* and *Wall Street Journal* daily but he spent the bulk of his time writing and poring over research material. He did indulge in cigars, sometimes while soaking in a cold tub and working on his research. Voegelin and his wife had no children, and while he described himself at various points in his life as a "pre-Nicaean Christian," a "pre-Reformation Christian," and a "Christian humanist," he did not belong to a formal church.[17]

One gets a sense of Voegelin's importance from the thoughtful scholars who have attempted to explain his significance. George Panichas writes that "In death, as in life, Eric Voegelin remains a spoudaios, a mature man; a sophos, a sage; and above all, the aristos phylax, the best guardian, of a civilized world of reason, dignity, and order."[18] Lewis P. Simpson called him a "Clerk," by which he meant, quoting Herbert M. Read, "intellectuals who devoted their lives to unworldly causes, the cultivation of the mind and spirit."[19] Gerhart Niemeyer stated that "Eric Voegelin has guided us to an understanding of what is the character of our time, through his clear distinction between ideology and philosophy, Gnosticism and order."[20] Ellis Sandoz described Voegelin and his work in this way:

> [Voegelin is] a man of vast learning, great intellect, courage, energy, and stamina, one whose subtle humor and imaginative insight enliven the encyclopedic range of his work with the vitality of present truth and the excitement of new vision. Tough-minded, devastating in oral debate and written critique alike, unflinching in exposing fallacies, charlatanism, and murderous intent of ideologues of all stripes, Voegelin is yet both fiercely unsentimental and supremely sensitive to the movement of the spirit in all its guises, to the positive force of reality through whose beneficence man's existence is gently graced with hope, goodness, and a modicum of order. He has mastered life as the practice of dying, and old age finds him serene. This is simply to say that Voegelin is a philosopher and we can remain his debtors because he has so loved the divine wisdom.[21]

What shapes and animates Voegelin's works is the same problem that influenced the work of other twentieth-century thinkers like Irving Babbitt, Walter Lippmann, C. S. Lewis, T. S. Eliot,[22] Aleksandr Solzhenitsyn, and Albert Camus.[23] In their own way each of these thinkers was responding to the Western crisis as a spiritual crisis; Solzhenitsyn's Harvard Address in 1978, "A World Split Apart," is the classic exposition of this insight. What is interesting to note about the diagnosis of these thinkers is not only that they classify the problem as spiritual but that they resist the conventional view that because the totalitarian societies of the Cold War are so corrupt, Western societies are spiritually healthy. Voegelin, like Solzhenitsyn, recognized a common element in the disorder of the West and the East. The spiritual disorder of the East and West may have been manifest in different ways but its source was fundamentally the same; the ideological deformations that were engendered in the Age of Enlightenment.

Voegelin's analysis of the Western crisis began with the recognition that the crisis had been identified by a variety of thinkers, beginning in the eighteenth century. In one sense the crisis dated back to Scotus Erigena in the ninth century and the Trinitarian speculation on history by Joachim of Fiore (Flora) in the twelfth century.[24] The crisis of the West, then, spanned a thousand years, and for at least three hundred years a significant body of literature was produced to identify and explain it.

Thus, as Voegelin stated, "[O]ne cannot deny that the theorists of decline on the whole have a case" (*NSP*, 128). But two factors separated Voegelin's analysis of the Western crisis from most of the eighteenth- and nineteenth-century thinkers that he discussed. First, Voegelin was writing from the vantage point of a late-twentieth-century thinker. The eighteenth- and nineteenth-century thinkers were faced with the difficulty of understanding the crisis from the perspective of its earlier stages. They understood that it was a spiritual crisis but they did not have the advantage of witnessing the effects of scientism or the advanced displacement of Christianity. In particular, they did not have the advantage of seeing the crisis culminate in the form of totalitarian mass murder. Second, Voegelin's response to the crisis of de-divinization was not to divinize man or murder God, as was the case with modern thinkers like Marx and Nietzsche. Voegelin's therapeutic response was not an ideological system at all, but rather openness to the transcendent ground of being. Unlike the eighteenth-century thinkers who recognized the modern crisis, his response was not a rejection of classical and Christian philosophy but a reconstitution of philosophical insights provided by representatives of the Mediterranean tradition like Plato, Aristotle, Augustine, and Aquinas.

CHAPTER TWO

THE CRISIS OF THE WEST

DISCUSSION AMONG SCHOLARS, social critics, and political leaders regarding the crisis of the West has been common enough in the twentieth century, but its characterization and corresponding analysis have been variegated. What causes confusion, especially in the United States, is the overwhelming success of the West in defeating foreign enemies like Nazi Germany and Soviet Russia, and the West's remarkable progress in natural science, technology, economic production, and material wealth. It is difficult for some to even imagine that under these conditions a crisis can exist that endangers the very survival of the Western political and social order. Such claims are likely to be considered alarmist, hyperbolic, or extremist, and are consequently dismissed. The reaction to Aleksandr Solzhenitsyn's Harvard Address is a case in point. Solzhenitsyn, like Voegelin, identified widespread spiritual disorder in American and Western life. For him, as for Voegelin, social disorders such as crime, drug use, high divorce rates, and rampant materialism reflected man's alienation from transcendence and the general belief that human happiness can be achieved without submission to a higher authority than human desire. In response to Solzhenitsyn's comments, First Lady Rosalynn Carter expressed her disappointment in his characterization of American culture. In a speech to the National Press Club she commented that "Alexander Solzhenitsyn says that he can feel the pressure of evil across our land. . . . Well I do not sense that pressure of evil at all." She added: "I can tell you flatly: the people of this country are not weak, not cowardly and not spiritually exhausted."[1] Leading newspapers like the *New York Times* and *Washington Post* also opined that Solzhenitsyn misunderstood American culture.[2]

Voegelin, like Solzhenitsyn, had to contend with those who denied that twentieth-century social disorder was symptomatic of a deeper civilizational crisis. He also faced the problem that many who acknowledged that the crisis existed mischaracterized it by failing to identify its spiritual roots. Indeed, talk of a spiritual crisis is typically regarded as unfitting for a progressive liberal society in which spiritual life is treated as a matter of personal choice that has no place in public affairs. Many cultural critics seem unwilling to consider the connection between institutional crisis and spiritual breakdown. Consequently, their analysis and prescriptive response is shaped by the very ideological factors that cause the crisis.[3] Many liberal intellectuals object to totalitarianism but fail to realize that their own ideological disposition shares a common ground with communism and Nazism.[4] This commonality prompted Voegelin to state, "The true dividing line in the contemporary crisis does not run between liberals and totalitarians, but between the religious and philosophical transcendentalists on the one side and the liberal and totalitarian immanentist sectarians on the other side" (*PE 1953–1965*, 22).[5]

Voegelin's understanding of the crisis of Western culture can be further differentiated from that of others. For example, to him the crisis is more than a problem of cultural literacy or dysfunctional political and social institutions.[6] As disturbing as it may be that Americans in particular, and Westerners more generally, have been alienated from their cultural and political heritage, the essence of the crisis is spiritual; it is a religious crisis. Political and social policies cannot effectively treat the current crisis unless they are shaped and accompanied by the truth of man's spiritual existence. For the crisis is a loss of the first order, one that threatens the very meaning of the Western world; its consequences are nothing short of that loss of consciousness of reality that leads in its most advanced stages to totalitarian mass murder and existential destruction. It is futile in such social and political conditions to focus exclusively on institutional remedies or democratic forms. Voegelin addressed the point in the context of discussing Plato's response to the disorder of Athens: "When the spiritual and moral disintegration of a polity has reached the phase of imminent destruction, the time has come for emergency measures that will supersede all constitutional forms. Plato understood that the nature and acuteness of the crisis required an extra-constitutional government of men . . ." (*OH III*, 215).

Many scholars and social critics have been able to identify the primary symptoms of the Western crisis—e.g., world wars, social disintegration, corrupt political leadership—but few have penetrated to its animating spirit like Voegelin. He traces the life of the crisis back to its historical, ideological, political, and existential conception rather than merely reacting to the visible symptoms in contemporary life with public policy recommendations or moral condemnation. The anxious rush to find immediate policy solutions to the crisis is itself part of the Western malady. There are intellectual and philosophical preconditions to the restoration of Western civilization. Voegelin spent a lifetime building a philosophical framework that could serve as the foundation for the recovery of order.

Characterizing the Crisis of the West

Voegelin does not mean by "the crisis of Western civilization" an "event that occurs at a definite point in time." Rather, "it is a process which extends by now over more than a century and a half and which, for all we know, may be protracted for another century. The crisis does not belong to the past, it is a living present. Every day adds to our experience of its extent and profoundness, and in the light of these experiences we are compelled, if we want to understand it, to revaluate the past phases of the crisis" (*FER*, 74). Voegelin's work does exactly that, bringing to light thinkers, ideas, and experiences that have contributed to the crisis. In this sense he provides the genealogy of the Western disorder, which requires that thinkers, ideas, and historical experiences that often have been given scant or improper attention by scholars be put in their proper context. An example of such a figure is Auguste Comte (1798–1857). Voegelin states that Comte "is the first great figure of the Western crisis" and he refers to him as "a spiritual dictator of mankind" (*FER*, 74–75). Along with other eighteenth-century figures like d'Alembert, Voltaire, Diderot, Bentham, and Turgot, Comte and his accomplices "have mutilated the idea of man beyond recognition." The mutilation is described by Voegelin as the "reduction of man and his life to the level of utilitarian existence" (*FER*, 95), an attitude that is ubiquitous in contemporary Western culture. This mutilation included the loss of the Christian understanding of mankind. According to Voegelin,

> There arises the necessity of substituting for transcendental reality an intrawordly evocation which is supposed to fulfill the functions of transcendental reality for the immature type of man. As a conse-

> quence, not only the idea of man but also the idea of mankind has changed its meaning. The Christian idea of mankind is the idea of a community whose substance consists of the Spirit in which the members participate; the *homonoia* of the members, their likemindedness through the Spirit that has become flesh in all and each of them, welds them into a universal community of mankind. (*FER*, 95–96)

Individuals like Turgot, Voltaire, Diderot, and Bentham transpose the classical and Christian idea of man in a way that depreciates man's spiritual nature. The spiritual community of individuals who share a likemindedness is transposed to a *masse totale*, in Turgot's ideological construction. In the utilitarian view, human beings have worth in proportion to their contribution to progress. The spiritual decay evident in this perspective gives rise to ideologies like positivism which create further spiritual corruption. The crisis is thus ultimately existential. Restoration, while possible, seems unlikely in the immediate future. The recovery of transcendent consciousness is difficult not only in totalitarian and formerly totalitarian societies but even in the U.S., where Voegelin noted that efforts at restoration must face "the soul-killing pressure of the progressive creed" (*FER*, 102). Yet Voegelin was adamant about the obligation to resist the spiritual crisis. "No one is obliged to take part in the spiritual crisis of a society; on the contrary, everyone is obliged to avoid this folly and live his life in order" (*SPG*, 22–23).

Unlike many scholars who recognize the crisis, Voegelin did not see "politics" as the solution. He explained that "we know today that the crisis is not a political disturbance, in the restricted sense of power politics, which can be settled by wars and subsequent peace treaties. We know that it is essentially a crisis of the spirit and we are acquainted today with some of the attempts at a solution of this problem through political religions such as National Socialism and Marxism" (*FER*, 74).

The diagnostic analysis of what has gone wrong is part of the prescriptive response that Voegelin provided. Knowing what deforms order helped to clarify what creates order. The deformation of order was, after all, the movement away from ordering experience, from the *realissimum* (the most real; the divine ground). Restoration, then, required movement back to the *realissimum*. The restoration was not a matter of returning to "the specific content of an earlier attempt" to restore order, but rather "a return to the consciousness of principles." And the objective was not a "literary renaissance of philosophical achievements of the past." Rather, "the principles must be regained by a work of theoretization which starts from the concrete, historical situation of the age, taking into account the full amplitude of our empirical knowledge" (*NSP*, 2–3). Restoration was not merely a matter of the recovery of historical symbols-experiences of transcendence. It required "the meditative reenactment of the motivating experiences of symbolic evocations of the past," which was a philosophical endeavor.[7]

The origins of the Western crisis, according to Voegelin, can be traced to the twelfth-century writings of Joachim of Fiore. Joachim of Fiore was "a twelfth-century Calabrian monk who founded a new religious order, [and] gave Western civilization the three-stage periodization of history which made possible the conceptualization of modernity itself. Joachim's division of history into the Ages of Father, Son, and Holy Ghost was the forerunner of Flavio Biondo's periodization of history into ancient, medieval, and modern eras, and of the Third Realm constructions in Condorcet, Comte, Marx, Lenin, and Hitler" (*NSP*, vi). Joachim created a "consciousness of epoch" (*FER*, 3)—an attitude that a new age had begun, that a new order had replaced the old order. In Joachim's case the new order was an immanentized (or entirely earthly) Christianity. Voegelin described the spiritual crisis as a loss of transcendent consciousness that began with Joachim's immanentizing historicism and degenerated centuries later into positivism's rejection of transcendent reality.

Voegelin pointed to two common misunderstandings regarding the Western crisis. First was the assumption that the crisis could be addressed by information about truth. The second was that a reform could "be achieved by a well-intentioned leader who recruits his followers from the very people whose moral confusion is the source of disorder" (*OH III*, 59). This second point was cause for sobriety about the possibility of restoration through political action—lawmaking, public policy, Supreme Court decisions. Drawing on Plato's political philosophy, Voegelin believed that political and social order could only be restored by ordering souls. "The disorder of society," he wrote, "is a disease in the psyche of its members" (*OH III*, 124). The quality of a political order reflected the ruling class's ethical character. "The true alternative would be the restoration of spiritual substance in the ruling groups of a society, with the consequent restoration of the moral strength in creating a just social order" (*FER*, 180). Voegelin thus placed his hope for restoration in philosophy, not politics, for it was philosophy that had the capacity to regenerate political leadership and in turn political and social order.

Philosophy was especially important in ordering the souls of the ruling class. But philosophy must be properly understood. "Philosophy is not a doctrine of right order, but the light of wisdom that falls on the struggle; and help is not a piece of information about truth, but the arduous effort to locate the forces of evil and identify their nature" (*OH III*, 117). Plato, for example, "does not offer recipes for moral conduct; and with regard to a right paradigm of life he does not go beyond a hint that in such matters the mean (*to meson*) is preferable" (*OH III*, 111). Philosophy is the resistance of the soul to disorder. A person whose soul is well ordered, like Plato, "can evoke a paradigm of right social order in the image of his well-ordered soul" (*OH III*, 123). This is the spiritual core of resistance to disorder and the beginning of the restoration of order.

What makes restoration difficult is the social strength of the crisis. Most individuals are not capable of ordering their souls and resisting disorder. Living a life of attunement to the transcendent in a disordered society is an act of great courage, and consequently, Voegelin discounted the possibility of a populist restoration. He noted, "Man is essentially social; to live in truth against appearance when the power of society is thrown on the side of appearance is a burden on the soul that is impossible to bear for the many, and hard to bear for the few" (*OH III*, 133). In a passage that seemed to describe the contemporary West, Voegelin added that "[t]he pressure for external conformity penetrates the soul and compels it to endow the *doxa* [opinion] experientially with *aletheia* [truth or *episteme*]. The last step would be the complete blinding of the soul by cutting off—through organized psychological management—the restorative recourse to the experience of transcendence as we find it in the modern political mass movements" (*OH III*, 133–134). This "last step" is, in Voegelin's evaluation, where the crisis of the West stands. In short, individuals are cut off from the experience of transcendence, or the divine, and the restoration of order requires the recovery of transcendent experience in human consciousness.

A major part of Voegelin's diagnosis of the Western crisis is his identification of thinkers who have contributed to this cutting off of the transcendent. The fear of philosophy is the result of Marx and Engels being "afraid that the recognition of critical conceptual analysis might lead to the recognition of a 'total context,' of an order of being and perhaps even of cosmic order, to which their particular existences would be subordinate" (*FER*, 260–61). Voegelin clarified this point by commenting that "[o]ur analysis has carried us closer to the deeper stratum of the Marxian disease, that is the revolt against God" (261). Marx's work was, consequently, "devoid of theoretical meaning" but "brimming with revolutionary pathos" (263). It attracted revolutionary-minded individuals who were impatient with the world as it is and who were looking for a solution to all social problems. Marx offered an ideological system that was legitimate only if its ideological dogmas were accepted. His work was not theory in the sense that Plato's political philosophy was theory; it was "pseudological speculation" (264).[8] That is, there was a logical or rational component to Marx's theory, but it was logical speculation about a fragment of reality that purported to be the whole of reality. In that sense Marxism did not describe an ontological reality; it created a false myth. Marxism could not be verified by human experience, but rather constructed a second or pseudo-reality that, if accepted, took on a life of its own with real political and social consequences. As a result, acceptance of Marxist doctrines was the end of rational discussion. There was no philosophical ground on which to discuss Marx's claims; the claims were themselves the ground and beyond critical discussion. The pseudological speculation of Marx and Engels included the idea that "'freedom,'" as Engels explained, "'consists in the domination of man over himself and external nature that is based on his knowledge of natural necessity.' The freedom of man advances with technological discoveries." Engels pointed specifically to the development of the steam engine as an important technological discovery that would transform human existence. This absence of philosophical clarity, combined with the immanentizing of Christian eschatology, was absurd; as Voegelin stated, "Christ the Redeemer is replaced by the steam engine as the promise of the realm to come" (267).

It should be emphasized that Voegelin's treatment of the Western crisis was realistic but hopeful. The final chapter of *The New Science of Politics*, for example, is titled "The End of Modernity." Some readers of his work are apt to characterize it as "pessimistic" —or "negative," to use the contemporary parlance. There is no doubt that in diagnosing the Western crisis Voegelin did not engage in a euphemistic description of the problem. If anything, he overstated the influence and scope of the crisis. Yet efficacious solutions are not possible unless the problem is accurately diagnosed, and though other scholars may provide superior prescriptions, effective responses to the modern malady are impossible without addressing the spiritual disorder that Voegelin identified.

Another important point regarding Voegelin's response to the Western crisis is that he did not advocate a return to a golden age of the past that can be engendered by a resurrection of great literary texts. He made clear that restoration did not mean a "literary renaissance" in the sense of studying great books. The objective of restoration was a transformation of consciousness that oriented and attuned the soul to the divine ground of being. This meant that restoration was not a matter of the intellectual acceptance of the specific content of past representations of order, as if they were dogmas (*NSP*, 2). Such a return to the past was unrealistic, if not undesirable. It would require the recreation of the historical and cultural conditions in which a particular state of political and social order existed. The short-lived glory of Athens, for example, was not something that could be replicated in other historical contexts. The true, the good, and the beautiful must be rediscovered and reconstituted in each historical age.

If this is the case, then what relevance does the past have for the contemporary search for order? What makes the past a living force on the present is the equivalent structure of consciousness that is the same in all historical settings. Because human nature is permanent and the process of discovering reality equivalent, previous discoveries of truth can illuminate the present search for order by directing the search for the divine ground of being. Voegelin explained that "all experiences of the divine ground are in like manner experiences of participation, even though they may considerably differ from each other on the scales of compactness and differentiation. . . . The equivalences of the symbols thrown up in the stream of participation, finally, leads to the loving turning back to the symbols belonging to the past, since they express phases of that same consciousness in the presence of which the thinker finds himself" (*A*, 158–59). It is this quality of consciousness that Voegelin sees as fundamental to the restoration of order. The specific language symbols that are used to express the state of consciousness should not be confused for their animating spirit. Language symbols are important because they are the shell that preserves the spirit, but they are not the ordering force itself. The symbols are evocative; they invite a search for the spirit and state of consciousness that engendered them. The recovery of order is a matter of spiritual awakening which requires the imaginative imitation of past experience, because that experience embodies the spiritual substance that orders the soul.

Specific accounts of truth are bound, in some respects, by the historical circumstances that engendered them. As historical circumstances change, specific language symbols may lose their relevance to contemporary life. But this does not mean that transcendent reality has changed. Rather it means that universality is preserved not in the content of symbols but in their engendering experience, an experience of the divine Beyond. The presence of the divine Beyond in historical experience is absorbed by the open soul that searches for its light. What is gained is the spiritual strength to resist disorder, not an ethical blueprint or rule of conduct. The literary content of past expressions of truth may or may not be relevant to the contemporary quest for the good society. But what is always relevant to the quest for order is the spiritual substance that lives in historical experience and waits to awaken the spiritually sensitive soul that seeks its nourishment.

The reality of differentiation—that is, the penetration to a deeper understanding of reality—also makes a return to the dead past as opposed to the living past impossible. Differentiations can be derailed but they cannot be undone. For example, we cannot undo the differentiation represented by Christianity and return to that state of consciousness and politics that existed in the pre-Christian West. Voegelin discusses this problem in the context of the differentiation in the Israelite order of history and its relation to the world-transcendent God. "History, once it has become ontologically real through revelation, carries with it the irreversible direction from compact existence in cosmological form toward the Kingdom of God" (*OH I*, 518). What can be done is to restore the understanding of truth about order that, although derived in various historical circumstances, contains an element of permanence and universality that, as a living force, can order souls and illuminate truth about reality.

CHAPTER THREE

THE HISTORY OF POLITICAL IDEAS

FOLLOWING THE COMPLETION of his five early books (*On the Form of the American Mind*, *Race and State*, *The History of the Race Idea*, *The Authoritarian State*, and *The Political Religions*) Voegelin entered what can be considered a new and second phase of his scholarship, one that corresponds to his emigration to the United States and his work on the *History of Political Ideas*. His escape from the Nazis and the experience of totalitarianism in Europe had provided the immediate context for his early work, but after coming to the U.S. his next major project was the result of Fritz Morstein-Marx's attempt to get him to write an introductory political theory textbook for McGraw-Hill.[1] The commercial objective was to produce a text to compete with the standard textbooks for political theory at the time: George H. Sabine's *History of Political Theory* (1937) and William A. Dunning's three-volume work.[2] Voegelin worked on this project which eventually evolved into his multivolume *History of Political Ideas,* from 1939 to 1954.

Significant differences separate Voegelin's *History of Political Ideas* from Dunning's and Sabine's works.[3] Their encyclopedic and descriptive approach eschewed theoretical analysis and critical judgment, which was at the forefront of Voegelin's approach to political philosophy.[4] Consequently, they failed to address the crisis of the West and its spiritual dimensions. For Voegelin, historical material was worth analyzing only because it was relevant—and, for Voegelin, the criterion for relevance was the provision of insight into the universal quest for order and the crisis of the West in particular. As he would later state in *The World of the Polis,* "[M]ankind is not constituted through a survey of phenomena by even the most erudite historian, but through the experience of order in the present under God" (*OH II*, 82). Education was for Voegelin the Platonic art of *periagoge,* the turning of the soul to the divine ground and away from the spiritual indolence and desolation of the world (*PE 1966–1985,* 22). The *History of Political Ideas* is written with this conception of education in mind.

Voegelin began to work his way through historical sources, starting with the ancient Greeks, as a way of constructing a study of political ideas that would go beyond descriptive history and address the spiritual dimensions of the Western crisis. He found the project to be much more involved than he initially thought. It required that he trace historical sources back to their intellectual roots, which required new language skills such as Hebrew and Chinese, and it became clear that starting the *History of Political Ideas* with the Greeks was untenable. As Voegelin explains: "The theory of the polis evocation has almost the character of an impasse, and the main current of ideas flows from Assyrian, Egyptian, Persian, and Jewish evocations through the Hellenistic period into the empire evocations. . . . The historic account has to begin, therefore, at least with the early empires of the Near East, and a good point could even be made for starting with an analysis of more primitive stages of human society, because their traces can be found in the later history" (*HPI I*, 235–236). Voegelin was intent on letting his work be directed by "the lines that connect one evocative situation with another." These lines of connection would provide meaning to the historical development of ideas and provide a structure to Voegelin's project. "To bring out carefully the connecting lines seems to be the most important task, because otherwise the history is in danger to degenerate [*sic*] into a collection of essays on important theoretical achievements that are not held together by anything but the covers of a book" (*HPI I*, 236). The organization and analysis of the study of political ideas in this way is one of the essential aspects of Voegelin's study of political ideas, and one that differentiates it from works like Sabine's and Dunning's.

Years passed and the unpublished manuscript mounted to more than four thousand pages.[5] In 1975 the final part of the *History*, Voegelin's work on the eighteenth and nineteenth centuries, was published under the title *From Enlightenment to Revolution*. No other volumes appeared in print until twenty-two years later (1997), more than a decade after Voegelin's death.[6] The decision to abandon the *History of Political Ideas* project came as the study was nearing an end and the analysis had reached the nineteenth century. Voegelin confesses:

> In the course of the work it became obvious that the limitation imposed on a history of ideas, the convention of having it begin with the Greek Classic philosophers and end up with some contemporary ideologies, was untenable. . . . I discovered that one could not very well write about the Middle Ages and their politics without knowing a good deal more about the origins of Christianity than I knew at the time, and that one could not properly understand the Christian beginnings without going into the Jewish background. . . . Through these studies on the Israelite background the pattern of a history of political ideas beginning with Greek philosophy had already exploded. . . . The background thus had expanded to the ancient Near Eastern empires from whom Israel emerged, the Israelites were the background for the Christians, and the Christians were the background for the ideas of the Middle Ages. The pattern of a unilinear development of political ideas, from a supposed constitutionalism of Plato and Aristotle, through a dubious constitutionalism of the Middle Ages, into the splendid constitutionalism of the modern period, broke down. (*AR*, 62–63)

His understanding of this problem is further articulated in *The World of the Polis*, the second volume in the *Order and History* series. There he states that one can trace the origins and evolution of constitutionalism in the works of Plato and Aristotle, for example, but only if one is misleadingly selective with the historical material.[7] Thus, *Order and History* is not only an alternative approach to the conventional history of constitutionalism but a rejection of it, for Voegelin believed that mode of historiography ignored the science of order on which Plato and Aristotle based their diagnosis of disorder in Athens. If for the purpose of creating a history of constitutionalism, their paradigms of order are separated from their engendering science of order, then those paradigms will be misconstrued as early forms of constitutionalism. In fact, Voegelin argued, the theoretical creation of a best polis has meaning only insofar as it is seen as the outcome of a philosophy of order that accounts for the decline and restoration of order (*OH II*, 98–99). Plato's conception of history, that "[r]estoration of order could only come from the soul that had ordered itself by attunement to the divine measure" (*OH II*, 109), is the critical insight missing from historical analysis that focuses exclusively on institutions or ideas. Viewed in this context, the classical exploration of what constitutes the best polis should not be considered the beginning of constitutionalism or a step in the historical development of the best type of political system, for the study of order and history is not primarily about finding the right ideas or institutions for creating the best regime. Rather, historical experience with order and its symbolic expression reveal a level of transcendent consciousness that can be regained and serve as a living force on the contemporary world. The institutional forms that best serve the needs of order and justice cannot be determined apart from this state of transcendent consciousness and order in the soul. Omitting an analysis of Plato and Aristotle's understanding of the life of the soul and transcendent consciousness from an account of their theory of the development of political institutions obscures the contribution of Greek philosophy—especially Plato's anthropological principle—to the history of mankind and the struggle for order through attunement.

Adding to Voegelin's decision to abandon the project was his realization that "the conception of a history of ideas was an ideological deformation of reality. There were no ideas unless there were symbols of immediate *experiences*" (*AR*, 63). That is, Voegelin realized that ideas should not be treated as "objects of a history" (*AR*, 80). The realization that the project was untenable did not occur at once; the critical point was reached in 1951 while Voegelin was preparing the Walgreen Lectures that subsequently were published as *The New Science of Politics*. Thus began the third phase of Voegelin's work. From this point on he would emphasize the importance of experiences with transcendence as the ordering force in political societies. To discover these experiences it is necessary to understand the symbols that are created to articulate them: "The men who have the experiences express them through symbols, and symbols are the key to understanding the experiences expressed" (*AR*, 80). Ideas can become separated from their engendering experiences and as independent entities become deformed in one of two ways. The first type of deformation is reification into dogma or doctrine. The second type is abstraction, which deprives ideas of their foundation of meaning. Furthermore, the ideas, once separated from their experiential roots, are subject to ideological reconstructions. The proliferation of "isms" in the nineteenth century represents a variety of fragments of reality that are considered by their proponents to be the whole of reality. An idea is, in other words, once or twice removed from the primary substance of reality, i.e., the engendering experience. Once formulated in this way, it becomes apparent that ideas are not the core of reality but malleable constructions of varying clarity. In Voegelin's terminology, ideas detached from experiential reality are "second realities" (*PE 1966–1985*, 36–51). Experience, then, is a much more reliable foundation for a philosophical study of political order. (There are drawbacks to Voegelin's position that experience has primacy over ideas, doctrines, and dogmas. Chapter 7 will take up this issue.)

Voegelin's abandonment of the *History of Political Ideas* project led to its being eclipsed by his *Order and History* project.

But the recent publication of the *History of Political Ideas* volumes has renewed interest in it and may change its perception. It bears repeating that one of the reasons for Voegelin's obscurity is that he did not write for the unprepared reader. His later work is especially difficult for the novice. Simply following Voegelin's arguments, to say nothing of critically examining them, requires a grasp of historical and philosophical material that most individuals do not possess. But the *History of Political Ideas* volumes have the advantage of being more accessible than Voegelin's later work, especially the last two volumes of *Order and History*.

The genuine contribution of the *History of Political Ideas* to Voegelin's scholarly corpus is readily apparent. Voegelin attempts to shift the focus of political science and analysis away from power and institutional mechanisms to the spiritual foundations of political and social order. The focus of the *History of Political Ideas* is explained by Voegelin in the introduction:

> To set up a government is an essay in world creation. Out of a shapeless vastness of conflicting human desires rises a little world of order, a cosmic analogy, a cosmion, leading a precarious life under the pressure of destructive forces from within and without, and maintaining its existence by the ultimate threat and application of violence against the internal breaker of its law as well as the external aggressor. The application of violence, though, is the ultimate means only of creating and preserving a political order, it is not its ultimate reason: the function proper of order is the creation of a shelter in which man may give his life a semblance of meaning. (*HPI I*, 225)

It is precisely this "shelter function" and the concomitant search for meaning in political and social community that Voegelin emphasizes in the *History of Political Ideas*. Voegelin follows the Aristotelian method of political science by beginning his analysis with the self-interpretative symbols of a particular society—for example, "justice," "happiness," "citizen." Once these symbols have been understood they must be measured against the political philosopher's language symbols. It may be that the "truth" as expressed by a society's self-interpretative symbols is at odds with the "truth" of the political philosopher. In this case the political philosopher is himself at odds with the society and lives in tension with it. What the political philosopher has to say about the order of society and justice may make the leaders and people of that society uncomfortable and insecure. The truth that the political philosopher offers is often rejected because the path it illuminates is beyond the existential strength of the society. The consequences for the political philosopher, in such circumstances, range on a continuum, from death, as in the case of Socrates, to simply being ignored.

The search for meaning in history leads Voegelin to a study of the particular attempts in various societies to "rationalize the shelter function of the cosmion" (*HPI I*, 225). These rationalizations, as a whole, make up the history of political ideas. They are the place, so to speak, to search for the self-interpretations of thinkers who have struggled to understand the meaning of their existence. Political ideas, in other words, reveal the meaning of history as understood by the individuals who experience it. Voegelin adds that while "[t]he scope and the details of these ideas vary widely . . . their general structure remains the same throughout history, just as the shelter function that they are [destined] to rationalize remains the same" (*HPI I*, 225–26). The purpose of language symbols is to "constitute reality," which for political ideas means evoking "a political unit, the cosmion of order, into existence" (*HPI I*, 228–29).

"Evocation," "shelter function," and "cosmion" are interconnected concepts essential for understanding Voegelin's arguments in the *History*, as they provide a framework for his analysis of political ideas. Voegelin begins his introduction to the *History of Political Ideas* by explaining the process by which political order is created out of what appears to be nothing but meaningless disorder. The "little world of order" that politics creates suggests that individuals who create that politics and live in it are aware of its existence and consequently face the problem of survival and all that it implies. But unlike Hobbes, Voegelin does not reduce politics, human psychology, or the human condition to the mere struggle for survival. Meaning, at least to some extent, is something that can be discovered in historical existence; in fact, the ultimate *raison d'être* for political societies is not mere existence or mere survival but the search for order and meaning (*HPI I*, 225). The search for order and the corresponding search for meaning that define the shelter function create the substance of history. The shelter function of the cosmion, however, not only occurs in history but must be "rationalized" through the use of political ideas. The process of rationalization is intended to provide meaning to what would otherwise be a meaningless existence. The search for order and meaning and its expression can be found in three kinds of ideas: "ideas concerning the constitution of the cosmos as a whole; the ideas concerning the internal order; [and] the ideas concerning the status of the cosmion in the simultaneous world and its history" (*HPI I*, 226). That is, political ideas are created to rationalize the shelter function of the cosmion.

By "evocation" Voegelin means that the political society as cosmion is called into existence. "The primary purpose of the political idea is to evoke a political unit, the cosmion of order, into existence; once this purpose is achieved, the cosmion is a real social and political force in history. . ." (*HPI I*, 229). In this sense, political ideas are not a "description of a political unit but an instrument of its creation." Evocation, then, is the act of calling a political unit and its parts into existence, and it is this aspect of political ideas that Voegelin refers to as the "evocative power of language." The "primary function of the language symbols involved in political ideas is to constitute reality. . ." (*HPI I*, 228). That is, although ideas can be used to describe reality or even to cloud human perception of it, Voegelin emphasizes the function that political ideas play in *constituting* reality. It is because of this ability that political ideas become destructive when they take the form of utopian dreams. For utopian ideas effectively attempt to abolish the cosmion by transforming human nature.

Once a political cosmion is evoked—that is, once a polity has come into existence—quite obviously it does not last forever. Why? Voegelin argues that the political ideas used to evoke the polity can lose their grip or evocative power. As he explains, "When the magic has lost its spell and the facade of government becomes transparent, the disillusioned observer can discover nothing but acts determined by tradition . . . and interest and lust of power. And disenchantment, having reached this stage, gives rise to a spirit of revolt against an unjust, crudely materialistic state of things" (*HPI I*, 230).[8] This description applies to several historical examples that Voegelin discusses in the *History of Political Ideas*, but it has its greatest relevance when applied to the Western crisis. He concludes the introduction to the *History* by addressing the issue of new evocations in the West, which can be interpreted as rejections of the existing period of "radical nationalism." "[S]uspicion is growing that the idea of the national state may be decaying and that, for at least two centuries, new types of evocation are developing slowly but distinctly" (*HPI I*, 237). If Voegelin is correct, the historical era of nation-states that seems so embedded in Western political consciousness may be entering its final stage of historical life. In other words, Western civilization may have reached its zenith and is now experiencing a process of long, slow decline.

A history of political ideas must at some point confront the issue of historical meaning. Voegelin was consistent throughout his work in insisting that the ultimate meaning of history is a mystery unknowable to human understanding. In the *History of Political Ideas* volumes he has harsh criticism for those, like Hegel and Marx, who claim otherwise. But that does not mean that history or the historic development of political ideas is meaningless. While "no single line of evolution can be drawn from a beginning point to the present" (*HPI I*, 233), "long periods of history are covered by the same basic types of evocation. . . . And every evocative process has to cope with the same basic problems, lines of tradition, and elaboration of theoretical problems . . . running from one evocative period to another. The internal process within an evocative period, and the process of tradition from one period to another, will furnish the rough general structure of the history" (*HPI I*, 235).

Indeed, this is clear when reading the *History of Political Ideas* volumes. One does not get the sense that unconnected ideas and historical events are being explored but rather that they are interconnected in a way that explains how the Western political and social order has evolved. Voegelin demonstrates how contemporary ideas are not possible without their historical antecedents and he traces continuous streams of thought in a way that emphasizes the seminal and politically formative aspects of the history of ideas. For example, Marx is not possible without a range of thinkers like Voltaire, Helvètius, Comte, Bakunin, Hegel, and Feuerbach. Providing the historical and the ideological context for a particular thinker's ideas illuminates the ideological commonality between thinkers who are part of the same intellectual tradition. It also allows Voegelin to demonstrate important connections between seemingly unrelated thinkers. One such example is Mark of the Gospel and Karl Marx (*HPI I*, 157). The relationship between gnostic thinkers like Marx and Christianity is parasitic. Marx takes from Christianity; he saps the spiritual life from it and ultimately displaces it with Marxism—the existence of Christianity and its death are necessary for Marxism to live.[9] Marx's concept of "emancipation" is a deformation of the Gospel idea of "*metanoia.*" Rather than a transformation of the soul, as is the case with *metanoia*, Marx posits a social transformation that is based on material conditions. Understanding the theoretical connections between Christianity and Marxism in this regard helps illuminate the meaning of modern ideas like "social justice" and why they are the products of souls that have lost their sense of authentic Christian spirituality.[10]

One of the more intriguing parts of the *History of Political Ideas* is the section on Cicero. Voegelin's evaluation of Cicero's political ideas is not what one might expect given Cicero's reputation in Western history as a great statesman and thinker. Voegelin depreciates Cicero's reputation in a way that helps explain why Voegelin considers conservatism and traditionalism to be secondary ideologies. It also illustrates the originality of his analysis in the *History* and his commitment to philosophical searching as opposed to political statesmanship. Voegelin begins his criticism of Cicero by stating that

> his clearness is a clearness of formula, not of thought; not only is he not an original thinker, but he expressly refuses to be one; going to the bottom of a problem is not an occupation for a gentleman, active in politics, but the affair of a "schoolmaster." His work is entirely devoid of the sublime unclearness of a great mind wrestling with his problem, fanatically engaged in his search for the structure of reality, happier to find a problem than to solve one. There are no problems in Cicero; whenever there is one insolent enough to come near the surface, the firm hand of the Roman consul and imperator comes down and bends it under the yoke of his authoritative language. (*HPI I*, 131)

In short, Cicero is not philosophical. He is too concerned with politics to engage in genuine philosophical thought. This is evident from his two dialogues, *Republic* and *Laws*, both superficial imitations of Plato's works. "Cicero is not Plato; his *Republic* does not create a polis out of the powers of his soul, and his *Laws* marks not a new level of spiritual development, but is simply a second volume dealing with subject matter that was not covered in the first" (*HPI I*, 132). Plato is a true philosopher because he identifies the spiritual crisis of Athens and penetrates to the existential core of the problems of order. He recognizes the flaws in the Athenian order and seeks to rectify them in his soul. Cicero, by contrast, has no need to create a best regime or identify the flaws of Rome because "Rome is the ideal state; all he has to do is to describe the constitution and the civil and religious law of Rome. . . . Rome is the ideal materialized" (*HPI I*, 135). The role of the political philosopher, however, is to recognize the inadequacies of the existing order. Politics can never fully realize the paradigm of order created by the philosopher, but it is nonetheless the duty of the philosopher to create tension between the order of the city and the order of the philosopher's soul. Cicero refuses this task. For Cicero, Rome is so great that "no inquiry into the material or spiritual conditions of the existence of a political community is either desirable or necessary." The consequence of Cicero's political theory is that the problems of politics are approached "only within the framework of an existent government." This approach ignores what Voegelin considers central to politics and political science: "the emotional and mythical structure of a political community." Moreover, Cicero's approach to political order has led to two widespread misconceptions in the contemporary Western order: "law is the basis of political society" and "the true government is possible only by consent of the governed" (*HPI I*, 136–137).

Cicero's idea of law as the foundation for politics and political analysis ignores the problem of evocation that gives rise to law. The engendering evocation that precedes the creation of legal institutions reveals the field of meaning in which human beings represent themselves in the larger order. Legal conventions are at least one step removed from the engendering evocation and thus cannot be, by themselves, the complete horizon of political reality. Because Cicero fails to penetrate to the highest philosophical level, as a political theorist he is inferior to thinkers like Plato or Heraclitus, who were, by contrast, deeply philosophical, widening "the gulf between the philosopher and the mass" (*OH II*, 303).

CHAPTER FOUR

THE SCIENCE OF POLITICS

The New Science of Politics was published at the critical juncture between the *History of Political Ideas* and *Order and History*. It provides an outline for *Order and History* and it links Voegelin's work on the *History of Political Ideas* to the development of his philosophy of consciousness. As such it is a good introduction to Voegelin's political theory. *The New Science of Politics* is also Voegelin's attempt to restore political science to its original meaning. In this book Voegelin questions the positivist foundation on which much modern scholarship rests and proposes the restoration of the classical science found in the political thought of Plato and Aristotle.

To restore political science in its classical sense it was first necessary for Voegelin to explain why positivism is not an appropriate foundation for the study of politics. Positivism is inadequate for two primary reasons: it subordinates the search for truth to methodology and it is closed to transcendent reality. Voegelin also explains why classical assumptions about politics are superior to these positivist assumptions. In providing such an argument Voegelin does not so much create a *new* science of politics as much as he provides the framework for a restoration of classical political science in a modern context. His hope was that such a framework would free the study of politics from the grip of ideological systems. Positivism is one of these ideological systems—and to the study of politics the most inimical.

In *The New Science of Politics,* Voegelin also critiques the foundations of liberalism, which he finds in the works of Hobbes. For Voegelin, Hobbes is representative of modern thinkers, who typically eliminate the transcendent basis of social and political life in their theoretical analyses. The result is the primary misconstruction of modern liberal thought: the attempt to create a political and social order that has no grounding in ethical reality. Whatever Hobbes and other liberal thinkers may argue, matters of the soul are inextricably bound up with the political and social order. Removing the transcendent source of order from political science does not change the ontological reality that Plato explained by way of the city and soul parallel, for the anthropological principle that Plato differentiates is a central part of the human condition. It is not an opinion that theorists can take or leave based on personal preference. Hobbes nonetheless attempts to remove the *summum bonum* from political life. Doing so requires that at the level of theory something must replace the transcendent ground as the orienting force for existential and social order.[1] As Voegelin formulates the matter in his analysis of Hobbes: "With the [removal of the] *summum bonum* . . . disappears the source of order from human life; and not only from the life of individual man but also from life in society; for . . . the order of the life in community depends on *homonoia*, in the Aristotelian and Christian sense, that is, on the participation in the common nous. Hobbes, therefore, is faced with the problem of constructing an order of society out of isolated individuals who are not oriented toward a common purpose but only motivated by their individual passions" (*NSP*, 180). In Hobbes, the common passion that orders political and social life is fear; the *summum bonum* is replaced by the *summum malum*.

The Nature of Scientism and Its Genealogy

"Scientism" is an ideology grounded on the assumption that facts can be distinguished from values.[2] In this view, facts are derived from the scientific method, whereas values are the product of uncritical human constructions (opinions) such as religion, tradition, and prejudice. The fact-value distinction assumes that reality can be known by fragmenting it from the universal whole to which its parts belong. Once separated from the whole and viewed as objects, facts are classified as empirical knowledge. If liberated from the constraints of values and properly grounded in scientific method, human reason is capable of discovering empirical truths instrumental not only to material progress, but also to political and social progress. Just as the *summum malum* replaced the *summum bonum* in Hobbes's political thought, in scientism scientific reason and the corresponding scientific method replace *nous* and *homonoia* as the community-forming substance of human nature. In the scientific view, political and social progress is predicated on the idea that the scientific method provides a universal standard for the discovery of truth. Scientifically derived truth, then, provides a body of knowledge that is the foundation for political and social consensus. All humans are assumed to be rational and equally capable of both using the scientific method and understanding the knowledge that results from its implementation.

Conflict in human society is due to differences of opinion, a confrontation of values. Scientism claims that the scientific method can eliminate such conflicts because it provides a "scientific" understanding of reality on which all rational individuals can agree. Once the scientific method is widely utilized, differences of opinion—and the corresponding political and social conflict that is caused by them—will wither away. That is, disagreement and conflict will disappear in the same way that they do among mathematicians who present mathematical proofs. Given an accepted body of mathematical principles and methods, either the proof works or it fails. In the process of discovering mathematical truth, there is no place for opinion or subjective judgment. The structure of mathematical reality, represented by mathematical principles and laws, is fixed and is taken as a given. Erroneous application of principle is possible but the principles themselves are not matters of opinion. Once the truth or failure of the proof is established, there is no basis for disagreement.

Francis Bacon, Thomas Hobbes, and René Descartes influenced the early development of positivistic scientism in important ways.[3] Bacon, in particular, promoted the notion that the scientific method was the foundation for a new civilization. Proper use of the scientific method would purge an individual's mind of unscientific influences and lead to the acquisition of knowledge. Bacon therefore provided the theoretical foundation for the scientific revolution. But the social and political implications of this view, while recognized by Bacon, were more explicitly developed by Hobbes and later positivists like Saint-Simon and Auguste Comte. The ideological doctrine common to all aspects of the positivist movement was that the scientific method could lead to increasingly complete human domination of nature and that subsequent dramatic social, political, and economic transformation would occur.[4]

But the historical development of positivism was not without its problems. As positivism developed and fueled industrialization, material progress occurred, but the anticipated social and moral improvement proved to be illusive. One reason for the lack of moral progress was that positivism undermined the existing Judeo-Christian moral foundation of Western culture. The rational-scientific approach of the early positivists had the effect of displacing Christianity in public life. Of course, the theoretical incompatibility of positivism and Christianity is apparent. The metaphysical elements of Christianity, which recognize the existence of a transcendent reality, cannot be reconciled with the methods or principles of positivism. Furthermore, positivism's destructiveness was augmented by the fact that it emerged in Western history at a time when the engendering experiences of Christian faith were losing their cultural strength. As a result, Western society had become vulnerable to emerging ideologies. In particular, it could not withstand the pressure from Newtonian materialism. Voegelin explained, for example, the effect of the publication of Newton's *Philosophiae naturalis principia mathematica* (1687): "To a spiritually feeble and confused generation, this event transformed the universe into a huge machinery of dead matter, running its course by the inexorable laws of Newton's mechanics. The earth was an insignificant corner in this vast machinery, and the human self was a still more insignificant atom in this corner" (*HPI VI*, 164). Christian faith in metaphysical reality, in the unseen realm of life, lost its vitality under the pressure of Newton's mechanistic physics.

According to Voegelin, the process of displacing Christianity had two phases. The first was "despiritualization," or the destruction of Judeo-Christian consciousness. But individuals were then open "to respiritualization from non-Christian sources," including radical political ideologies like nationalism, humanitarianism, biologism, and psychologism. Later positivists like Saint-Simon and Comte filled the spiritual void with a new intramundane religion of humanity in which they assumed the roles of priest, prophet, pope, and god-incarnate. The religious positivists, like Comte, took the movement to its final stage and pushed the Western crisis to a new level of spiritual deformation. The early positivists removed spiritual matters from the purview of science; the later positivists filled the spiritual void with immanentizing political religions.[5] Voegelin explains the displacement of Christianity by modern political ideologies in terms of language symbols being separated from their experiential roots. Rationalism "destroys the transcendental meanings of symbols taken from the world of the senses. In the course of this 'de-divinization' (Entgötterung) of the world, sensual symbols have lost their transparency for transcendental reality; they have become opaque and are no longer revelatory of the immersion of the finite world in the transcendent." Christian symbols became "opaque" as a result of "the active center of intellectual life" shifting "to the plane of our knowledge of the external world" (*FER*, 21–25). As a consequence, the symbols of transcendent reality lost their relevance to public life and meaning or were judged by utilitarian criteria. They were not considered as expressions of truth about reality. Once Christianity lost its authoritative and unifying place in Western civilization, the spiritual void could be filled by the pseudo-religions of modern ideology (*FER*, 3). Viewed in this historical and philosophical context, scientism is both a deformation of reality and part of a larger historical movement that contributed to the loss of transcendental consciousness. It is a major part of the disorder of the modern age.

Criticism of Scientism

Voegelin identifies the eighteenth century, the Age of Enlightenment, as the proper historical context for understanding scientism. Three aspects of the Enlightenment are particularly important in this regard: "a denial of cognitive value to spiritual experiences," "the atrophy of Christian transcendental experiences," and the attempt "to enthrone the Newtonian method of science as the only valid method of arriving at truth" (*FER*, 3). The consequence of these Enlightenment dogmas was the fusion of two assumptions: first, that the methods of the mathematizing sciences are inherently superior to other methods and that the success of the natural sciences could be duplicated by other areas of science if they utilized these methods; second (and most dangerously), that the methods of the natural sciences were the measure for theoretical relevance in all areas of science. The combination of these two assumptions resulted in a series of common assertions: "[A] study of reality could qualify as scientific only if it used the methods of the natural sciences, that problems couched in other terms were illusionary problems, that in particular metaphysical questions which do not admit of answers by the methods of the sciences of phenomena should not be asked, that realms of being which are not accessible to exploration by the model methods were irrelevant, and, in the extreme, that such realms of being did not exist" (*NSP*, 4).

While scientism is open to truth and the existence of an objective material reality, it is closed to the spiritual reality of the inner life experienced through participation in transcendence and expressed symbolically through myth, revelation, history, and philosophy. While positivists like Comte certainly include spiritual matters in their work, it is not a transcendent spirituality but a secular-immanent spirituality, a pseudo-spirituality.[6] As Voegelin explains, in the positivistic view "[t]he horizon of man is strictly walled in by the facts and laws of the phenomena; . . . If gods exist, they certainly are not permitted to participate in history or society." The positivists manifest an existential unwillingness to engage in the search for transcendent reality, an aversion to philosophy that Voegelin calls "logophobia" (fear and hatred of philosophy). The political and social consequences of positivist logophobia include the destruction of human consciousness of the Agathon (the Good), which in turn severs the connection between the order of the soul and the order of the political community.[7] In short, politics loses its transcendent foundation.

The Restoration of Science

Voegelin recognizes scientism as one of the primary obstacles to the restoration of Western civilization. In *The New Science of Politics* he contrasts scientism with Aristotle's *episteme politike*. Voegelin points out that Aristotle's political science begins by examining symbols as they occur in reality (*NSP*, 34). All societies create symbols to express their place in the larger order of reality. "Elaborate symbolism" is used to express the meaning of society, including its place in history and the cosmos. This process of self-interpretation provides human beings with a sense of the abiding and permanent aspects of life, which are the basis for a just social and political order. But the self-interpretative symbols that articulate experience with transcendent reality are precisely what modern positivism attempts to exclude from scientific discovery.[8] Because a society's elaborate symbolism takes the form of rite, myth, and theory—and because its content is metaphysical experience—such symbols fail to meet the positivist definition of scientific fact. Consequently, what Voegelin considers "an integral part of reality" isn't real at all in the eyes of the positivist. Yet, as he explains, "when political science begins, it does not begin with a *tabula rasa* on which it can inscribe its concepts; it will inevitably start from the rich body of self-interpretation of a society and proceed by critical clarification of socially pre-existent symbols" (*NSP*, 27–28). Voegelin's creation of a new science of politics is meant to recover human experience with metaphysical reality, to establish the process of this recovery as scientific, and to restore human consciousness of metaphysical reality.

"*Nous*" is an example of a symbol whose recovery can help restore human consciousness of nonmaterial reality. Differentiated by Plato and Aristotle as the awareness of a divine presence in human consciousness, *nous* is akin to right reason in that it is the ability to understand truth. That is, in the classical view, human understanding of truth requires the participation of the divine in the process of knowing. But *nous* is not a tangible object in the external world, and thus to the ideology of scientism it is not part of reality. For Voegelin, however, it is real because it is experienced. Experience of *nous* verifies its ontological existence. In this sense historical experience, not the scientific method, is the standard by which to judge the truth of theoretical arguments.[9] Symbols such as "*nous*" or "*xynon*"[10] are articulations of experiences with transcendence that can be rediscovered because the presence of *nous* or *xynon* is a universal feature of human nature. Skeptics are likely to argue that *nous* is not universal because they have not experienced its presence in their consciousness. But acceptance of Voegelin's argument about science and the scientific validity of symbols like "*nous*" and "*xynon*" depends on an openness of will and imagination toward the transcendent reality he discusses. Failure to accept philosophical truth is not a problem of insufficient intellectual power but a problem of existential orientation. Scientism is incompatible with Voegelin's philosophical approach because the former begins with imaginative and existential closure, what Voegelin sometimes calls "estrangement," to transcendent reality; scientism refuses to engage in the philosophical search for higher truth (it is logophobic). Consequently, as with Marxists, open discussion is impossible with positivist ideologues because they cannot get beyond their ideological dogmas; they are unwilling to put aside the propositions of scientism, which are obstacles to open discussion. All ideologies prevent the search for truth.[11]

Voegelin applied this understanding of ideology to democratic theory, explaining the consequences ideologies have for a democratic order. Contrary to the tenets of pluralism, now widely accepted in Western democracies, Voegelin claimed that democracies "can be tolerant only toward those who are willing to submit to the conditions of the civil government" (*PE 1953–1965*, 62). Political groups that subscribe to antidemocratic principles that are at root closed to transcendent reality are destructive to democratic order. Voegelin believed that under certain circumstances, like those that prevailed during the Weimar

Republic, such political factions should be prohibited from participating in the democratic system.[12]

Voegelin's new science of politics shows that restoration requires that gnostic ideologies be seen for what they are, and that souls that have been closed as a result of their influence be opened by the renewal of experiences with—and insights about—transcendence.[13] Restoration cannot occur unless a consciousness of transcendence exists.

The methodology of positivism, which determines theoretical relevance based on method rather than subordinating method to the search for truth, is also problematic. Voegelin considers this a perversion of the meaning of science. Properly understood, "science is a search for truth concerning the nature of the various realms of being. . . . Facts are relevant in so far as their knowledge contributes to the study of essence, while methods are adequate in so far as they can be effectively used as a means for this end. Different objects require different methods." Thus, Voegelin argues that if "the use of a method is made the criterion of science, then the meaning of science as a truthful account of the structure of reality, as the theoretical orientation of man in his world, and as the great instrument for man's understanding of his own position in the universe is lost" (*NSP*, 4–5).

Representation

Besides Voegelin's refutation of scientism and his attempt to restore political science to its classical meaning, he also provides an analysis of representation that demonstrates the new science of politics. To the conventional modern mind, representation connotes primarily institutional representation in accordance with a constitution, or what might be called political representation. Voegelin calls this type of representation "elemental representation." Members of the U.S. Congress are representatives in the elemental sense. Elemental representation is a political structure that provides the people who are governed with a voice in the affairs of government. As part of the institutional structure of government it pertains to the process of government. For example, representatives are lawmakers. They create, debate, authorize, and oversee the law. While the elemental aspect of representation is important—it is in fact essential—it is neither the only aspect of representation nor the most important. Moreover, elemental representation cannot be understood in isolation from other aspects of representation. Institutional aspects of government do not exist or function independently of the human search for meaning and self-understanding. Another way to express this point is to recall Voegelin's use of the concept "shelter function" in the *History of Political Ideas*. There he explains that governments and political societies come into existence not simply to provide for material needs like self-preservation but primarily to give life meaning (*HPI I*, 225). This search for meaning includes an articulation of a political society's place in the larger order of the cosmos. Physical survival requires political institutions, like representation, that equip a society for action in a world that includes the challenges of economic production and distribution, national defense, and public safety. But accompanying the needs of physical survival and material well-being is the need to orient the self and society to the larger universal order. This aspect of representation Voegelin calls "existential representation."

Those interested in the more "practical" and institutional side of politics may wonder why existential representation should be a concern for those primarily interested in the day-to-day affairs of governing and politics. Voegelin explains, "If a government is nothing but representative in the constitutional [elemental] sense, a representative ruler in the existential sense will sooner or later make an end of it. . ." (*NSP*, 49). In other words, the problem of physical survival is connected to the problem of existential representation. If political rulers and representatives ignore the problem of existential representation, a void of meaning is created that provides an opportunity for leaders who are prepared to provide such representation. In other words, directing a society's attention exclusively to self-interest and the pragmatic concerns of survival does not eliminate the problem of existential representation. Rather, it makes it more likely that individuals of intemperate minds will become the existential representatives.

Another reason why Voegelin's analysis of representation is important relates to the form of government. "Goodness," he explains, "is the quality of a society and not of a governmental form" (*PE 1953–1965*, 186). The good society can take many different shapes. No one form of government is best or ideal in all circumstances. In a discussion of the classical concept of the good society Voegelin remarks that "[t]he model of the good society is not an a priori datum. Its construction is extremely elastic and must vary with our empirical knowledge of human nature and society. One sure thing is that the social effectiveness of the life of reason, which is constantly developing, must be included" (184). Now it has become a generally accepted proposition in the West that democracy is the best form of government and that something like democratic capitalism ought to be exported around the globe. The primary consequences of global democracy are those articulated by Woodrow Wilson: increased international peace and prosperity. The recent advocates of global democracy, however, pay little or no attention to the problems of existential representation. They assume that a sound political order will follow the creation of democratic institutions—an assumption that has been often proved wrong—and give scant thought to the cultural and existential requirements for democratic government. By contrast, Voegelin states that "[d]emocracy is possible only where civic virtue exists. And the first of virtues, without which all others lack a proper basis for action, is sound knowledge of the principles of social coexistence among free men in a free society" (*PE 1953–1965*, 59–60). Self-government requires a people to have cultural maturity. Western societies have the historical experience that prepares them for democratic institutions, but this is certainly not the case for every society. Indeed, Voegelin considers democratic government to be a "specifically Western form of political order" (65), one not always appropriate to a particular people's need for existential representation. Failure to address the problem of existential representation is one of the primary components of the Western crisis. He explains why it has consequences in practical politics: "Our own foreign policy was a factor in aggravating international disorder through its sincere but naïve endeavor of curing the evils of the world by spreading representative institutions in the elemental sense to areas where the existential conditions for their functioning were not given" (*NSP*, 51).

The contrast between Voegelin's thought and today's conventional liberal internationalism and its support of global democracy is readily apparent here. To the latter way of thinking liberal political institutions are appropriate for all societies regardless of their cultural maturity or historical experience. Voegelin, by contrast, explicitly raises such questions as, What is the best institutional approach for a society that does not have the existential conditions for constitutional government? He notes that John Stuart Mill understood that constitutional government was only possible in societies that had sufficiently developed the life of reason and rational debate. With specific reference to the twentieth century, Voegelin adds:

> Unconscionable damage to millions of people throughout the world has resulted from ill-considered constitutional experiments modeled after the West. It is imperative that we face the facts. Not all societies are good, and the attempt to imitate the Western type entails revolutionary changes that can perhaps only be brought about by dubious means. . . . We must admit that constitutional democracy may be a terrible form of government for an Asian or African country, whereas some form of enlightened despotism, autocracy, or military dictatorship can be the best if we believe that the rulers are using this means to try to create a good society. (*PE 1953–1965*, 186–187)

Gnosticism

Gnosticism plays a critical role in Voegelin's analysis of modernity, as indicated by his statement in *The New Science of Politics* that "the essence of modernity" is "the growth of Gnosticism" (*NSP*, 126). While Voegelin would later modify this claim, the gnostic character of modernity remained a primary feature in his analysis of modern consciousness.

Drawing on and expanding his analysis of gnosticism in *The New Science of Politics,* Voegelin provides an extensive characterization of gnosticism in *Science, Politics and Gnosticism.* There he argues that gnosticism is engendered by dissatisfaction with the world as it is, which leads to the desire to transform the world through political action. This basic ideological structure of gnosticism is prevalent in modern politics. It is the imaginative substance and existential disposition that engenders both liberal and radical progressivism. It can also be found in strains of romantic conservatism. Voegelin identifies six primary characteristics of gnosticism:

1. Dissatisfaction with the current situation.

2. Belief that the dissatisfactory aspects of the current situation are the result of the world being poorly organized.

3. Faith that the situation is not hopeless; "salvation from the evil of the world is possible."

4. Belief that for salvation to occur, the constitution of being (i.e., human nature and the structure of reality) has to be transformed in history.

5. Belief that the transformation of the order of being is possible through human action, especially political action.

6. Because the transformation of the order of being is

> possible and humans can initiate and direct it, belief that a plan or formula for doing so must be created based on gnosis, the secret knowledge that unlocks the mystery of the order of being and allows the leaders of the gnostic movement to reorganize the world in a way that transforms the order of being. The result is the transformation of social, political, and existential reality. The gnostic plays the role of the prophet who reveals the ideological formula for salvation. (*SPG*, 86–87)

The ultimate goal of gnosticism, the transformation of the order of being and society, is also referred to in Voegelin's terminology as the immanentization of the Christian eschaton. In Christianity and gnostic ideologies there is a parallel movement from the fall to the ascent. The Christian, however, anticipates the ascent, the movement toward human perfection, as a movement out of history in the Beyond, whereas the gnostic conceives of this perfection of man as an event in history. Voegelin states that "the structure of history is empirically nonapocalyptic" (*PE 1953–1965*, 152). There is no escape from the metaxy (the permanent structure of existence) in history. Humans are forced to confront the challenge of attuning their souls to the transcendent. Spiritually indolent individuals, those whose souls are not "ordered by faith," look for ways out of this difficult and unpleasant reality. The anxiety of life that Pascal identifies as *noirceur* is a "blackness that pervades the soul, the emptiness that results in boredom and ultimately in despair" (*PE 1953–1965*, 50). Escape from boredom and despair comes in the form of diversions (what Pascal called *divertissements*) like narcotic intoxication, television, and music, or it may be found in gnostic ideologies that transform the problem of attaining virtue to one of political action and faith in ideological doctrines. Resistance to these gnostic impulses is more difficult in a culture whose genuine spiritual capital has been depleted (*PE 1953–1965*, 50).

Voegelin's understanding of gnosticism provides a framework for analyzing the Western crisis. The ideological components of modernity—National Socialism, Marxism, progressivism, scientism, and other "isms"—are manifestations of gnosticism. They are spiritual disorders and the political corruption that they create is the outcome of existential disorder. Confronting the modern crisis means providing an alternative to gnostic attitudes. But this is made difficult by the fact that the various gnostic ideologies have so corrupted human consciousness that to many the only palatable alternative to ideology seems to be pluralism. Unfortunately, placing all ideologies on an equal playing field with genuine philosophy is not likely to help resolve the modern crisis. The gnostic ideologies not only have a unique advantage in that they promise things that humans crave—salvation and perfection—but also in that they promise to deliver them in this world. The impatience and idealism of the modern personality make the Christian promise of life after death or the sober Augustinian view of a world rife with sin unappealing by comparison.

But Voegelin does not view the modern age as a gnostic rout. Gnosticism has certainly destroyed much of the civilizational fabric of the West, but it has not gone unchallenged. Voegelin is one in a long line of thinkers who have resisted the gnostic impulse and defended the Mediterranean tradition from its enemies. He repeatedly reminds readers that "it must never be forgotten that Western society is not all modern but that modernity is a growth within it, in opposition to the classic and Christian tradition" (*NSP*, 176). He also explains that "in spite of its noisy ascendancy, [gnosticism] does by far not have the field for itself; . . . the classical and Christian tradition of Western society is rather alive; . . . the building-up of spiritual and intellectual resistance against gnosticism in all its variants is a notable factor in our society; . . . the reconstruction of a science of man and society is one of the remarkable events of the last half-century and, in retrospect from a future vantage point, will perhaps appear as the most important event in our time" (*NSP*, 165). With the help of other thinkers who sought to restore classical and Christian philosophy, including Vico, Bodin, Schelling, and Bergson,[14] Voegelin was confident that gnosticism would run its course and that a spiritual revival would occur. He commented that "nothing lasts forever! We'll get a religious revival; it will come" (*CEV*, 109).[15]

Voegelin's confidence that the modern crisis would eventually dissipate was based in part on his belief that gnosticism, the animating ideological force of the crisis, was self-defeating. One aspect of the self-defeating character of gnosticism is that "its disregard for the structure of reality leads to continuous warfare" (*NSP*, 173). The wars are inspired by gnostic dreams that can never be realized because they are premised on second reality. At some point, individuals lose their patience waiting for dreams to come true. This is especially the case when the anxiety of the wait is exacerbated by totalitarian terror. Thus, in time the falsehood of the gnostic dream is exposed. It loses its vitality under the pressure of reality; common sense eventually prevails, at least in a civilization that has a living philosophical tradition, as is the case in British and American culture. As long as this civilizational capital is not entirely spent, the cultural substance to resist gnosticism exists.

One might wonder why gnosticism can have such influence if, in the end, it is apt to be exposed as a pathological dream. Why isn't gnosticism seen for what it is right from the start? Voegelin rejects the idea that gnostic politics, for example, can be explained by "ignorance and stupidity" (*NSP*, 172). Gnosticism is not a return to a "Dark Age" of unthinking ignorance. Gnostic politics and its accompanying policies are "pursued as a matter of principle, on the basis of Gnostic dream assumptions about the nature of man, about a mysterious evolution of mankind toward peace and world order, about the possibility of establishing an international order in the abstract without relation to the structure of the field of existential forces, about armies being the cause of war and not the forces and constellations which build them and set them in motion. . ." (*NSP*, 172). In other words, the crisis of the West, the ascendency of gnosticism as the civil theology of the West, is not caused by a rational miscalculation due to ignorance. Gnostic politics is propagated by intelligent individuals who suffer from "the strange, abnormal spiritual condition" that Voegelin, following Schelling, terms "pneumopathology" (*SPG*, 101). He discusses the pneumopathological disorder of gnostics in *Science, Politics and Gnosticism* and in *The New Science of Politics*. In the former he uses Marx and Nietzsche as examples of "speculative gnostics" who engage in "deception" and who commit "intellectual swindles" (*SPG*, 28–33). In Voegelin's terms, the "movement of the spirit . . . in Nietzsche's gnosis corresponds functionally to the Platonic *periagoge*, the turning and opening of the soul." Gnostic spiritual "turning" or transformation is distinguished from Platonic or genuine spiritual transformation in that the latter is an opening of the soul to the transcendent source of order, whereas gnostic transformation is exactly the opposite. The gnostic soul closes itself off from the moving grace of divine love. As Voegelin explains, "The will to power strikes against the wall of being, which has become a prison. It forces the spirit into the rhythm of deception and self-laceration" (*SPG*, 30).

Voegelin's analysis of the existential disorder in the soul of gnostic thinkers is especially galling to the sensibilities of modern gnostics. Voegelin identifies the spiritual character flaws of gnostic thinkers, and his judgments are therefore apt to be interpreted as insulting, vituperative, or intellectually belligerent. Yet he explains that the evidence leads one to such a conclusion. Gnostic thinkers like Hobbes and Hegel "suppressed an essential element in reality in order to be able to construct an image of man, or society, or history to suit [their] desires." To understand why a thinker would engage in such intellectual dishonesty requires that the analysis of the problem move from "theoretic argument" and reason to "the psychological level." It is then on psychological grounds that Voegelin determines that "the will to power of the gnostic who wants to rule the world has triumphed over the humility of subordination to the constitution of being" (*SPG*, 106–107). In short, the gnostic thinker refuses to accept the natural limits of man and society. For accepting these limits means giving up the dream of a transformed human nature and its social and political consequences.

The gnostic's suppression of reality must eventually collide with "the constitution of being." When it does, the romantic dream is exposed as nonsense. Yet the gnostic thinker can continue the dream in the face of reality because in doing so he achieves a "fantasy satisfaction." The will to power is not satisfied, but there is a "psychic gain" that results from gnostic constructions and the emotional investment its followers make in the "truth" of their ideological programs. A second psychological motivation lies in "stronger certainty about the meaning of human existence, in a new knowledge of the future that lies before us, and in the creation of a more secure basis for action in the future" (*SPG*, 107).[16]

Two conclusions are apparent from Voegelin's analysis of gnosticism. First, gnosticism and philosophy are at odds; they are irreconcilable tensions that result in equally irreconcilable existential and political orders. Philosophy is the love of knowledge that proceeds by an open quest for the good. The philosophical quest is itself directed by the transcendent ground, and man's search for truth is subordinated to God's will. Gnosticism, by contrast, is animated by the will to power, *libido dominandi,* or *amor sui*, the love of self (in Augustine's sense). The desire to dominate being is characteristic of gnosticism. Gnostics create systems that distort reality. But ultimately reality cannot be ignored or destroyed. The gnostic thinker avoids the problem by refusing to address questions that expose the untruth of the gnostic construction.

The second conclusion is that gnostics are closed to rational debate.[17] This conclusion has important consequences for politics. It means that constitutional democracies, with all their protections for civil liberties like free speech, are undermined by gnosticism. Free and open speech does not ensure rational discussion. The open society is vulnerable to gnosticism because truth does not always prevail over untruth. Civil libertarians assume that free expression ensures the perpetuation of the free society. But gnostics do not want a free society; they want to reconstruct reality according to their gnostic dream. As Voegelin knew from his experience with totalitarianism, gnostics are not content with fantasy satisfaction; they crave power. He noted that the "*libido dominandi* . . . has a violence and cruelty that go[es] beyond the delight in masquerade and in the deception of others. It turns on the thinker himself and unmasks his thought as a cunning will to power" (*SPG*, 29). There is no guarantee that the gnostic's pathological dreams will be seen for what they are—witness Nazi Germany and the Soviet Union. A society may reach a point of spiritual confusion or spiritual corruption that destroys its ability to fend off gnostic advances. The difficulty for constitutional societies is that at the point when theoretical clarity is most needed, gnostic influences may have eroded the society's ability to make accurate distinctions between truth and untruth. Institutional openness is not in itself adequate to protect a society from gnosticism, nor is it likely to prevail at the point when gnosticism is culturally and spiritually pervasive (*PE 1940–1952*, 19–21). Thus, gnosticism must be opposed by a spiritual force that immunizes the society from gnostic corruption.

Gnosticism and the Movement from Compactness to Differentiation

For Voegelin, human understanding of truth can be measured on a scale that moves from compactness to differentiation. As human experience with transcendent reality occurs through history, new and deeper insights are gained about the nature of reality and the human condition: this is the essence of differentiation. It is important to note that while differentiation is a multifaceted process, experience with transcendent reality is its engendering substance. The insights that are gained and articulated into language are the consequences of experiences that Voegelin calls "leaps in being."[18] The leap in being "gains a new truth about order" but it is neither "all of the truth," nor does it establish "an ultimate order of mankind." Rather, "The struggle for the truth of order continues on the new historical level." Moreover, "Repetitions of the leap in being will correct the initial insight and supplement it with new discoveries; and the order of human existence, however profoundly affected by the new truth, remains the order of a plurality of concrete societies. With the discovery of its past, mankind has not come to the end of its history, but has become conscious of the open horizon of its future" (*OH II*, 69).

Differentiation does not guarantee a parallel improvement in political and social order. That is, differentiation involves the development of noetic reason (rational action in human science), but it does not guarantee a concomitant development in pragmatic reason (rational action in the area of natural science and technology in the external world) (*PE 1953–1965*, 187–188). An advance in noetic reason is relatively independent of rational action in natural science and technology, which is instrumental to economic development and national security. In fact, differentiation may undermine the existing civil theology and be inimical to the existing political and social order in the way that Socrates was disruptive to Athens.

Differentiation is by definition a new understanding of reality that moves a society away from its existing and more compact understanding of truth. But the more compact understanding is not thereby proven to be false.[19] Plato's philosophy does not invalidate the insights of Hesiod, but only constitutes a deeper level of understanding about the nature of reality. The "new" differentiated truth is not completely new; it builds on the insights of compact truth. In fact, less differentiated experiences share an equivalence with more differentiated experiences. New symbols are engendered to express new insights into the human condition, but the experiences are not new. They too come from human participation in the universal structure of reality. At the level of historical experience what one individual participates in is equivalent to what those before and after him have participated in, i.e., the *metaxy*. In the cases of both compact and differentiated truth the divine is recognized as the moving factor in human consciousness. The strength of the divine pull (*helkein*) and the human response to it (*zetesis*) may vary in particular cases, but in each instance individuals participate in the same process of discovering reality. Consequently, experiences with transcendent reality are not unconnected. They are connected by the common factor of the divine presence, the parousia.

The equivalence of experiences at the level of consciousness does not necessarily correspond to social and political continuity. Philosophers like Voegelin may be able to recognize the continuity between historical experiences with transcendent reality, but unlike philosophers, cultures tend to guard jealously their conventional representations of truth. Philosophical insights (differentiations) are culturally preserved in some form of civil theology. For most individuals the content of the civil theology, though in reality only derivative of differentiated truth, is taken as the truth itself. Further differentiation requires a new civil theology or reform of the old one. To the philosopher this change is not a rejection of the more compact truth, but to the common man it appears as truth's betrayal. Because the social and political order of a community, including its institutions, are a reflection of its understanding of the larger reality, further differentiation is bound to be disruptive to the existing order. Christianity had such an effect on Rome. Voegelin believes that St. Augustine, for example, was not sufficiently sensitive to Varro's complaint that Christianity, in undermining Rome's civil theology, was responsible for its fall. Roman civil theology was expendable as far as Augustine was concerned because it was not Christian, and civil theology itself was unnecessary in the aftermath of Christian differentiation.

Not only is differentiation generally apt to be socially and politically disruptive, but Christian differentiation in particular adds a further dimension to the problem of order. Christianity represents a universal truth relevant to all members of the human community, and this universality tends to have a displacing effect, in that Christianity holds that other religions are inferior and should be replaced. Moreover, Christianity rests on spiritually fragile ground. It is far removed from the certainty of cosmological symbols and myths that have points of identification in the visible world. The ordering center of life for the Christian is part of the unseen reality of spiritual existence and must be known through faith. The uncertainty of faith is prone to engender a quest for certainty that leads to the formation of reified propositions that are deformations of differentiated reality. Voegelin classifies the deformations of Christian differentiation as gnostic. Modern gnostic movements—Marxism, National Socialism, progressivism, positivism—"betray in their symbolism a certain derivation from Christianity and its experience of faith" (*SPG*, 114). In a certain sense, then, modern gnostic movements are not possible without the differentiation of Christianity because Christianity provides the context for modern consciousness. Modern gnosticism is a derailment of Christianity. Voegelin claims that gnosis "accompanied Christianity from its very beginnings" (*NSP*, 124); "its traces are to be found in St. Paul and St. John" (126).

An important question must be raised here. If differentiation does not result in a more just and ethical political and social order, why is it so important? The derailments of Christianity might lead some to the conclusion that the modern world, at least, would have been better off without it. Voegelin's point is not that differentiation necessarily has negative consequences for political and social order but that differentiation in itself does not guarantee moral improvement in social and political life. The differentiated truth can be rejected by the disordered society. But it can also be accepted. Voegelin discusses the social effects of differentiation in the context of contrasting the sophists with mystic-philosophers like Heraclitus and Xenophanes. The mystic-philosophers "have discovered a new source of truth in their souls" (*OH II*, 311), whereas the sophists have discovered only information to be offered for sale to a society in need of order. The mystic-philosopher

> can only communicate the discovery that he has made in his own soul, hoping that such communication will stir up parallel discoveries in the soul of others. If he has this effect on others, he will have actualized the existing community to the extent of his effects.

> Nothing follows from this adventure with regard to social organization directly, although indirectly the differentiation of the life of the soul in a great number of men in a community may have the effect of changing the mores, and ultimately the institutions of a society, because the hierarchy of purposes for individual action has changed. (*OH II*, 357)[20]

Even if rejected by a disordered society, the differentiated truth can have an ordering effect, but it may not be in that society or in that historical era. Although Athens rejected the truth discovered by Plato and Aristotle, they "created the new type of society that could become the carrier of their truth, that is, the philosophical schools. The schools outlived the political catastrophe of the polis and became formative influences of the first order, not in Hellenistic and Roman society, but through the ages in Islamic and Western civilizations" (*NSP*, 75). Viewed against the larger horizon of both Western and Eastern civilization, and taking into account Voegelin's concept of existential representation, the efforts of Plato and Aristotle were not wasted on a society that refused to follow their wisdom. Rather, they provided the civilizational and philosophical substance that animated the order of political societies centuries beyond the fourth century B.C.

The differentiation of Christian revelation and philosophy places certain limits on human consciousness that have contributed to the rise of scientism. "The truth of revelation and philosophy has become fatal to the intracosmic gods; and the removal of the gods from the cosmos has set a dedivinized nature free to be explored by science" (*OH IV*, 53). The dedivinization of nature makes scientism possible. Christianity also dedivinizes "the temporal sphere of power," which sets the stage for redivinization. "Modern re-divinization has its origins . . . in Christianity itself, deriving from components that were suppressed as heretical by the universal church" (*NSP*, 107). But there is no turning back from the differentiation of Christian revelation and philosophy—polytheism is no longer an option. The new insights into the human condition revealed by Christianity are embedded in human consciousness and cannot be removed easily, if at all. But they can be deformed. As Voegelin explains, "after Christianity one cannot go back to cosmology but only forward to a more differentiated understanding of the unity of mankind in history under the mystery of the eschaton . . ." (*PE 1953–1965*, 153). The differentiation of the Incarnation has identified "mankind as the subject of history" (174). Post-Christian differentiation has been prevented, however, by anti-Christian revolutionary movements that Voegelin classifies as "apocalyptic deformations of history" responsible for making "mankind" "a synonym for the inmates of an apocalyptic concentration camp" (153).

Joachim of Fiore (Flora) is an important figure in the redivinization of society. Voegelin believes that "[i]n his trinitarian eschatology Joachim created the aggregate of symbols which govern the self-interpretation of modern political society to this day" (*NSP*, 111). Joachim's division of history into three epochs in which the third and final epoch represents the end and fulfillment of history was the symbolic model for later modern thinkers like Turgot, Comte, Hegel, Marx, and totalitarian mass movements like National Socialism and communism. For Voegelin, Joachim's trinitarian eschatology is a defining characteristic of modernity and especially modern politics.

The gnostic characteristic of modernity is illuminated when compared to Augustine's understanding of history. For Augustine history has two components: the profane and the sacred. Profane history is the realm of history in which "empires rise and fall," whereas sacred history is the realm of history which "culminates in the appearance of Christ and the establishment of the church" (*NSP*, 118). Two important points need to be made about this distinction. First, Augustine understood that while the sacred realm of history was directed toward "eschatological fulfilment," profane history has no such purpose (*NSP*, 118). The second point is that modernity is defined, in part, by the confusion and melding of Augustine's two realms. Modern thinkers redivinize society by giving an eschatological meaning to profane history. "Joachim broke with the Augustinian conception of a Christian society when he applied the symbol of the Trinity to the course of history" (*NSP*, 111), explains

Voegelin. In other words, Joachim "immanentized the eschaton." Modern political thought must be understood in light of Joachim's effort and subsequent attempts to redivinize what Christianity had dedivinized.[21]

More generally, a frustration with the world as it is characterizes modern political thought and modern politics.[22] In the modern view, human nature and the structure of existence are considered to be not fixed but infinitely malleable; if only the right ideological mechanism can be brought to bear on them, like the proletarian revolution or racial purification, they can be perfected. The frustration characteristic of modernity can therefore be described as an unwillingness to accept the limits of reality, or what Voegelin calls the constitution of being. What results is the imaginative escape from reality in ideological understandings of the world that provide programs for social and political action. There is a stark contrast between the gnostic illusions that characterize modern political thought and Voegelin's philosophical realism. Here one finds a continuity between ancient thinkers like Plato and Aristotle and Christian thinkers like Augustine and Aquinas, all of whom understood that while improvements are possible in politics, earthly life is marred by the tendency of men to choose sin over grace, disorder over order, *doxa* over *episteme*; sophistry over philosophy. The metaxy—the structure of reality—is permanent and unchanging. But the eschatological transformation of society requires nothing short of a transformation of human nature and transformation of the metaxy itself. Hence, this aspect of modern political thought has a strong utopian flavor to it. "It may assume the form of an axiological dream world, as in the utopia of More, when the thinker is still aware that and why the dream is unrealizable; or, with increasing theoretical illiteracy, it may assume the form of various social idealisms, such as the abolition of war, of unequal distribution of property, of fear and want" (*NSP*, 121).

It may be helpful to explain why modern idealism is fundamentally different from the "idealism" of Plato or Aquinas. Voegelin once explained on a panel with Allan Bloom, Hans-Georg Gadamer, and Frederick Lawrence that Plato is not a utopian.[23] His ideal regime, as explicated in the *Republic,* is not perfect; it includes imperfections and degenerates into even "less perfect" forms and ultimately into tyranny. In other words, even the best regime has imperfections, and all regimes degenerate due to imperfections in human nature. Voegelin argues that "the title 'good society' does not contain any eschatological overtones; its establishment is not a final achievement that brings imperfect history to an end. Even the best of the good societies follows, according to the classical concept, the cyclical law of decline and fall; and corruption begins from the moment of its inception" (*PE 1953–1965*, 184). This is not to say that disorder and injustice always triumph over order and justice. What moral progress is gained can be lost and what is lost can be regained or reconstituted. Particular individuals and communities experience continuous dynamic changes from order to disorder or from disorder to recovery of order. But in the context of earthly human existence order and justice cannot prevail once and for all. To believe that disorder and injustice can be extinguished would be to reject the very ontological foundation of reality that is expressed in symbols like "metaxy," "constitution of being," and "human condition."

In this respect, then, Plato is not a utopian because he does not believe that perfection is possible.[24] A strain of modern political thought, by contrast, *is* utopian, in a way that distinguishes it from pre-Christian utopianism, of which Thomas More is an example. Voegelin discusses More's utopianism in the *History* and briefly in *The New Science of Politics* and *Science, Politics and Gnosticism*. More's utopianism differs from Marx's in that the former recognized that the dream is unrealizable while the latter not only thinks it can be realized, but also that the realization is historically inevitable. In both cases Christian differentiation and the gnostic element of Christianity feed the desire to immanentize the eschaton. In both cases the creation of utopian dreams results from pneumopathology. The pneumopathological thinker omits a part of reality in order to create the illusion that a radically new world is possible. Although More seems to understand that the structure of existence cannot be transformed to create utopia, he is nonetheless willing to engage in the imaginative exercise of constructing a world in which the obstacles to perfection have been removed. His utopianism may not be as pernicious as Marx's but it is part of the development of consciousness that contributes to more radical and dangerous forms of utopianism. It is an indication that by the early sixteenth century Western civilization was beginning to lose its grip on reality.

CHAPTER FIVE

PHILOSOPHY OF HISTORY: ORDER AND HISTORY

Before providing some description and analysis of *Order and History*, it is necessary to understand precisely what Voegelin means by history and order and why they are intimately linked for him. Voegelin states that "history is the process in which man articulates his own nature" (*OH II*, 68). History, then, is the discovery of self-understanding. And self-understanding is understood as knowledge and insight about the nature of human existence, which includes man's attunement to transcendent reality.

To be known and articulated, experience with transcendent reality must be part of human consciousness. For this to happen human beings must be attuned to transcendent reality, as opposed to being estranged from it. Attunement implies a certain ethical condition of the soul and a corresponding state of consciousness. When the will is rightly ordered, experiences with transcendence are illuminated, resulting in insights into the human condition and the meaning of history that build on each other. Three assumptions underlie this Voegelinian thesis. First, the structure of human nature is fixed. Second, "[t]he range of human experience is always present in the fullness of its dimensions." Human beings are capable of a range of personality types and a range of ethical behavior, like those described by Plato in the *Republic*.[1] Third, "[t]he structure of the range [of human experience] varies from compactness to differentiation" (*OH I*, 99). In other words, some experiences penetrate to a deeper understanding of reality than others, not necessarily because the thinker lacks intellectual or moral power, but because reality unfolds in history to varying degrees. While spiritually sensitive individuals participate in the process of unfolding, they do not create the structure of reality; they search for it and it is revealed to them. Consciousness of reality requires the union of the divine pull (*pneuma* or *helkein*) and the willingness to search for it (*zetesis*, *nous*, or Bergson's *l'âme ouverte*). The degree of differentiation is due not only to the spiritual and intellectual capacity of a thinker, but also to the strength of the divine pull.

The insights gained through human experience with transcendence and the order that they engender are part of the process of self-understanding that forms the substance of history. It is this understanding of history as the "struggle for the truth of order" that shapes Voegelin's philosophy of history (*OH II*, 68), giving his work both a different focus and a different substance than most conventional historical studies. For Voegelin, history is made when concrete human beings who are engaged in a political community participate in the dramatic struggle for order. The existential resistance to disorder in that community and the corresponding discovery of order in the soul is the very essence of historical existence.

In Voegelin's conception, history does not consist in the study of the past without regard for the philosopher's search for the truth of existence. Not all past events and experiences are historical, nor do they have equal relevance to contemporary problems of order. Consequently, critical judgement inspired by an openness to the ground of being must be used to determine what is historical. Moreover, the study of history should not be bound by ideological constructions like relativistic multiculturalism, dialectical materialism, or scientism, doctrines that are uncritical and closed to the ground of being. This understanding of history means that all societies do not play an equally important part in the drama of history. For that reason "a philosophy of history cannot be an amiable record of memorabilia" (*OH II*, 73) that gives equal attention to all civilizations and societies. "History is made wherever men live, but its philosophy is a Western symbolism . . . because Western society has received its historical form through Christianity" (*OH II*,

90). "[T]he truth about the order of being emerges in the order of history. The Logos of history itself provides the instruments for the critical testing and ranking of the authoritative structure" (*OH II*, 73). In a statement that draws on his *History of Political Ideas*, Voegelin explains that "[e]very society is organized for survival in the world and, at the same time, for participation in the order of being that has its origin in world-transcendent divine Being; it has to cope with the problems of its pragmatic existence and, at the same time, it is concerned with the truth of its order" (*OH II*, 68). These facets of human existence are the inescapable challenges that provide history with substance and meaning. The discovery of meaning in history is brought to clarity in the present, and thus history "is experienced not in the past but in the present" (*WIH*, 10).

With this unique historical vision as his foundation, Voegelin provides in *Order and History* an analysis of the "representative thinkers whose discoveries decisively advanced the understanding of the order of man and society" (*OH II*, 270). These advances are the discovery of transcendence—the "transcendent-divine order," as opposed to the more compact understanding of a "cosmic-divine order"—and the intellectual and spiritual order that occurs because of it. Such discoveries are naturally endowed with authority and have social significance. As Voegelin states, "[O]nce the discovery is made, it is endowed with the quality of an authoritative appeal to every man to actualize it in his own soul; the differentiation of man, the discovery of his nature, is a source of social authority" (*OH II*, 256–257). The recovery of order in the disordered society depends on the confrontation between the truth (*aletheia*) represented in the soul of its carrier and the disorder of society represented in the untruths or illusions (*doxai*) of the day. The representative thinkers who have discovered the *aletheia* that Voegelin discusses in *Order and History* should be viewed in this context; they have ordered their souls in accordance with the *Agathon* (the Good), and their resistance to *doxa* (disorder) is the path that society must follow to restore the *Eunomia*, the right order.

Israel and Revelation

In the preface to *Israel and Revelation*, the first volume in his *Order and History* series, Voegelin writes that "[t]he order of history emerges from the history of order."[2] Order is an inescapable problem for political societies and it is indissolubly bound up with the search for meaning. Great societies, "beginning with the civilizations of the Ancient Near East, have created a sequence of orders, intelligibly connected with one another as advances toward, or recessions from, an adequate symbolization of truth concerning the order of being of which the order of society is a part" (*OH I*, 19). Voegelin's study of order and history explains the "sequence of orders" and how they are "intelligibly connected." That is, the struggles for order in great societies are often comparable and even, at times, equivalent.[3] There is, Voegelin believed, an "intelligible structure of history." The unfolding of this intelligible structure of history is "a reality beyond the plans of concrete human beings—a reality of which the origin and end is unknown and which for that reason cannot be brought within the grasp of finite action" (*OH I*, 19–20).

Voegelin maintains that the origin and end of history is a mystery, an understanding of history that sets Voegelin's philosophy of history apart from the ideological constructions found in Hegel and Marx. Unlike those thinkers, Voegelin does not claim to have figured out the end of history. Nor is his philosophy of history offered as a means to transform human nature and human society. Human nature is fixed and constant, and the discovery of truth about the historical process and human nature will not necessarily have a positive effect on political and social order. Moreover, "Amnesia with regard to past achievement is one of the most important social phenomena" (*OH I*, 19). "The truth of order has to be gained and regained in the perpetual struggle against the fall from it. . ." (*OH I*, 24). New insights and their accompanying expressions can represent challenges to older understandings of truth and hence be politically disruptive. "The appearance of Plato did not change the course of the Hellenic crisis, the case of Nietzsche did not serve as a warning example for Germany nor did the appearance of Dostoevsky make a dent in the tsarist system" (*FER*, 180). Societies in spiritual crisis are the ones most likely to gain new and differentiated insights into the truth of human existence, but they also are not easily restored to order. It may be that the philosopher, poet, or prophet can save his own soul and a few others but the particular society in which he lives is beyond the point of recovery. Yet, as was indicated in chapter 4, this does not mean that differentiation is unimportant for restoring political order. For the ordering substance of differentiation (i.e., the engendering experience and its symbolic articulation) provides the philosophical capital with which new orders are created that come into existence long after the original differentiation occurs.[4] Whatever the case may be in a particular society, the struggle for existence and meaning provides an historical record of the search for order, which is especially relevant to a civilization, like the West, that is facing disintegration from within because it has lost touch with its meaning.

As extensive as Voegelin's historical analysis is, he maintains a sober view of what can be known about the unfolding of truth in history. He adamantly opposes what he calls "stop history" programs, which claim to have discovered the ultimate meaning of history and consequently declare its end. Hegel, Marx, and Francis Fukuyama are representative examples of this genre of historicism. Whatever may be said about history and human participation in it, "no answer [about the meaning of history] can abolish the historical process of consciousness from which it has emerged" (*OH IV*, 125). For Voegelin historical knowledge has a more sober utility.

Voegelin's sobriety contrasts with apocalyptic views of history, including the notion of metastatic apocalypse, i.e., "a transfiguration of reality through an act of faith" (*AR*, 68). Voegelin uses the terms "metastatic faith" and "metastatic apocalypse" to describe the prophecy of Israelites like Isaiah, who counseled the King of Judah "not to rely on the fortifications for Jerusalem and the strength of his army but on his faith in Yahweh. If the king would have true faith, God would do the rest by producing an epidemic or a panic among the enemy, and the danger to the city would dissolve." The king was astute enough not to follow this advice, but the dangerous idea had emerged that the structure of reality could be transformed by an act of faith (*AR*, 68; see also *OH I*, 502–509). While Voegelin recognizes the possibility of a "change in being" that changes order, he is careful to explain that it is not "a leap out of existence" (*OH I*, 49). Attunement to the divine ground of being experienced as conversion (the Platonic *periagoge*) is not an escape from the structure of reality but participation in and consciousness of it. Moreover, the problem of mundane existence remains until death for the individual and until political disintegration for the society. In short, differentiation does not change the nature of man. In the aftermath of differentiation, "Man still exists under God in the world, within the limits set by his nature, within society and history, with all the obligations and responsibilities such existence entails" (*PE 1953–1965*, 174).

Voegelin's philosophy of history is intended to serve as an intellectual and cultural countermeasure to ideologies of metastatic faith. Voegelin often draws this very contrast. For example, he concludes the preface to *Israel and Revelation* by noting that "[i]deology is existence in rebellion against God and man. It is the violation of the First and Tenth Commandments. . . . [I]t is the *nosos*, the disease of the spirit. . . ." Philosophy, by contrast, "is the love of being through love of divine Being as the source of its order." Voegelin draws a parallel between Plato's historical circumstances and the contemporary state of crisis. "[E]ver since Plato, in the disorder of his time, discovered the connection [between the diagnostic and therapeutic functions of philosophy], philosophical inquiry has been one of the means of establishing islands of order in the disorder of the age" (*OH I*, 24).

For the order of history to emerge theoretical analysis must focus on the experiences of order and the corresponding institutions of particular societies. The interpenetration of experiences of order and institutions creates a "form" that can be theoretically analyzed. Three such forms are the cosmological form, the historical form, and the philosophical form. As Voegelin argued in *Israel and Revelation*, Egyptian society is an example of a cosmological form, whereas Israel and Christianity are examples of historical forms (*OH I*, 165).[5] Historical form is only possible with the differentiation of the world-transcendent God, which forms the foundation for universal history. But the Israelites never reached the level of understanding that is the philosophical form (*OH I*, 286–87).

The movement or differentiation from one symbolic form to another—as was the case in ancient Greece in the movement from myth to philosophy—has implications for political and social institutions and order. For one thing, the differentiation is itself the result of resistance to societal disorder. The break with the mythical form occurs as a result of the discovery of the soul as the source of order rather than the cosmos (governed by the gods), which is identified as the source of order in the cosmological form. Myth is the symbolic form that expresses the experience of a cosmos "full of gods." Philosophy and revelation are symbolic forms that express the experience of the universe under a world-transcendent God (*PE 1953–1965*, 144). Moreover, the world-transcendent God symbolically articulated through philosophy and revelation is a universal transcendent God. Whereas the cosmological understanding of order relies on "the *visible*-divine order into which man must integrate his existence," philosophy and revelation connote a new understanding that places emphases on "the *transcendent*-divine order to which man must attune his existence" (*PE 1953–1965*, 144, emphasis added). Voegelin summarizes the importance of the differentiation from a *visible*-divine order to a *transcendent*-divine order in this way:

> Although they distribute the accents differently . . . they still are experiences of the same total structure of being: In the compact experiences of the cosmos ritual attunement to divine order is required as much as pragmatic adjustments to its visible order; in differentiated experience of the universe under God, pragmatic adjustment to the visible order is necessary as much as the attunement of existence to the "unseen measure." What is at stake in both cases is the truth of human existence, truth in the sense of a willingness both to understand and to accept the *condicio humana*—although it requires the advance toward the differentiated experience of transcendent Being in order to establish explicitly the insight that the order of the world is not of "this world" alone but also of the "world beyond." (*PE 1953–1965*, 144)

Recall that Voegelin believes that the ordering experiences and institutions of a society are inextricably bound up with one another. If new differentiated ordering experiences occur, then corresponding institutional changes are necessary to bring the institutions in sync with these experiences. "The discovery of transcendence, of intellectual and spiritual order, while occurring in the souls of individual human beings, is not a matter of 'subjective opinion'; once the discovery is made, it is endowed with the quality of an authoritative appeal to every man to actualize it in his own soul; the differentiation of man, the discovery of his nature, is a source of social authority" (*OH II*, 256–257). It may happen, however, that society rejects the differentiated experience and thus does not make the requisite existential and institutional changes. In such a situation, the existing compact symbolism will persist. Voegelin explains that "the symbolism will remain the same in time, if necessary through several millenniums, until the compactness of cosmological experience is broken through the opening of the soul to the revelation of God" (*OH I*, 340). Although differentiation does not guarantee social and political change, it does change permanently man's consciousness of truth. The movement from the compact symbolism of the cosmological myth to the differentiation of philosophy represents a new insight into the order of reality. With this differentiation the cosmos has become dedivinized. If the differentiation becomes socially vibrant, the new experience of order changes the civilizational form of the society.

Cosmological Symbolization and the Myth

Voegelin identifies three types of symbolizations of truth: cosmological, anthropological, and soteriological. The focus of *Israel and Revelation* is on the cosmological form of symbolization, defined by Voegelin as "the symbolization of political order by means of cosmic analogies" (*OH I*, 78). This form of symbolization draws connections to and integrates a society's social and political institutions with the order of the cosmos—that is, as the ordering force behind the rhythms of nature (e.g., the change of seasons, the cycle of vegetation and the patterns of planting seasons, tides, full moons, weather). In short, the visible part of the cosmos has an order to it that corresponds to natural laws that govern the physical universe. Cosmological symbolization "is the mythical expression of the participation, experienced as real, of the order of society in the divine being that also orders the cosmos. . . . [T]he cosmos and the political cosmion remain separate existences, but one stream of creative and ordering being flows through them. . . ." Both the cosmos and the political cosmion "are parts of one embracing order" (*OH I*, 66). Cosmological societies create symbols to express "the point of physical connection" between the cosmos and the political cosmion. Voegelin uses the Greek name *omphalos* to represent this class of symbols. He describes it as "the navel of the world, at which transcendent forces of being flow into social order" (*OH I*, 67). In Hellas the omphalos was the stone at Delphi, in China the symbol of a *chung kuo* (*OH I*, 67–69).

The discovery of order in the visible cosmos provides cosmological societies with a concrete reality that serves as the foundation for political and social order. However, just because the cosmos contains a foundation of order that orients the political and social life of particular societies does not mean that those societies consistently emulate the order of the cosmos. Political civilizations continually oscillate between order and chaos. Order is fleeting. The movement from chaos to cosmos—a movement from disorder to order—and then back again is so common in cosmological societies that Voegelin considers it a form. Indeed, the fall from order and the need for renewal is not limited to cosmological civilizations but is a universal problem of history. History is "the perpetual task to regain the order under God from the pressure of mundane existence" (*OH I*, 471). Indeed, the perpetual nature of this task is part of the tension of history that gnostics find unbearable. Thus, one of the characteristics of gnosticism is the belief that order can be restored permanently, that the movement from order to disorder can be prevented once and for all.

Another possible ideological deformation is metastasis. Voegelin explains that Isaiah "has tried the impossible: to make the leap in being a leap out of existence into a divinely transfigured world beyond the laws of mundane existence." Once the leap out of existence is conceived the existing world is juxtaposed to the transfigured world. The leap out of existence is, in Plato's language, an escape from the metaxy. The structure of existence and human nature have been imaginatively transformed. But, as Voegelin writes, "[t]he constitution of being is what it is, and cannot be affected by human fancies." The personality type who is prone to metastatic fits is in revolt against the divine. "The will to transform reality into something which by essence it is not is the rebellion against the nature of things as ordained by God" (*OH I*, 505–507).

Just as Voegelin claims that gnosticism was present from the beginning of Christianity, he argues that the roots of metastatic faith were present "from the very beginnings of the Mosaic foundation, in the conception of the theopolity as the Kingdom of God incarnate in a concrete people and its institutions" (*OH I*, 506). In fact, Voegelin traces a connection between the metastatic symbols of the Israelite and Jewish order through Christianity to modern gnosticism:

> While in the main development of Christianity . . . the metastatic symbols were transformed into eschatological events beyond history, so that the order of the world regained its autonomy, the continuum of metastatic movements has never been broken. It massively surrounds, rivals, and penetrates Christianity in Gnosis and Marcionism, and in a host of gnostic and antinomian heresies; and it has been absorbed into the symbolism of Christianity itself through the Old Testament, as well as through the Revelation of St. John. Throughout the Middle Ages, the Church was occupied with the struggle against heresies of a metastatic complexion; and with the Reformation this underground stream has come to the surface again in a massive flood—first, in the left wing of the sectarian movements and then in the secular political creed movements which purport to exact the metastasis by revolutionary action. (*OH I*, 508)

But there is an important difference between the metastatic dreams of the Hebrew prophets and the metastatic nightmares of modern gnostics:

> If the prophets, in their despair over Israel, indulged in metastatic dreams, in which the tension of historical order was abolished by a divine act of grace, at least they did not indulge in metastatic

> nightmares, in which the *opus* was performed by human acts of revolution. The prophets could suffer with God under the defection of Israel, but they could not doubt the order of history under the revealed will of God. And since they could not doubt, they were spared the intellectual confusion about the meaning of history. They knew that history meant existence in the order of being as it had become visible through revelation. One could not go back of revelation and play existence in cosmic-divine order, after the world-transcendent God had revealed himself. One could not pretend to live in another order of being than the one illuminated by revelation. And least of all could one think of going beyond revelation replacing the constitution of being with a man-made substitute. Man exists *within* the order of being; and there is no history *outside* the historical form under revelation. (*OH I*, 518)

The meaning of Voegelin's philosophy of history is illustrated by his use of terms like "myth" and "experience." Myth is connected to experience in that myth articulates an experience with transcendence. Voegelin further distinguishes between original experience and the imaginative reenactment of experience. The engendering experiences of transcendent reality would have limited importance if they could not be in some way re-experienced; to have social significance they must be evocative. Thus, imagination plays a key role in the reenactment of engendering experience, and this is the role of myth. It keeps engendering experiences with transcendent reality alive and vibrant, giving individuals the opportunity to relive those experiences with transcendence that order the soul.

Engendering experience with transcendent reality is not a common occurrence. It takes a rare and special kind of individual to be open to such experiences and to respond to them in a way that captures the fullness of the divine movement in the soul. "[R]eligious personalities who have such experiences, and are able to submit to their authority, do not grow on trees. The spiritual sensitiveness of the man who opened his soul to the word of Yahweh, the trust and fortitude required to make this word the order of existence in opposition to the world, and the creative imagination used in transforming the symbol of civilizational bondage into the symbol of divine liberation—that combination is one of the great and rare events in the history of mankind" (*OH I*, 241).

Voegelin's meaning of myth is best understood in the context of his specific historical discussions. For example, he discusses myth in the context of the creation story in Genesis. The account of creation articulated in Genesis is not intended as a literal account of the origins of the world. Voegelin explains that "[s]uch an account is not a body of propositions concerning events witnessed by a historian or, for that matter, by anybody. The stories of the Creation, of Noah and the Flood, of the Tower of Babel, and so on, are myths; and their 'subject matter' is not the content of the stories but the experiences symbolized by means of the stories" (*OH I*, 218). While the myth is not an account of events that someone witnesses, "the [genuine] myth embodies the truth of an experience" (*OH I*, 219). The conclusion that the myth about creation described in Genesis can be true but not an accurate description of how the physical world was actually created violates both the scientific and fundamentalist sensibilities of modern thinking. The very notion that a myth can in any important sense be true seems counter-intuitive to modern rationalism. Yet if Voegelin is correct, truth about transcendent reality cannot always be described in the same way that facts about material reality are explained. But the mythical form is one way that truth about such reality can be articulated. Philosophy is another. Whatever form the symbolization may take, what is primary to the process of differentiation is experience.

Voegelin explains that "the order of society and history participates in the order of God only in as much as the universal, transcendent God is experienced as such in the faith of men who order their existence in the light of their faith and thereby become the representative center of society and history" (*OH I*, 525). Yet success in the political realm is not necessarily an indication that a political community is attuned to the divine ground. This was an issue with which the Israelite prophets had to contend. Likewise, if the problem of order is metastatized, as with Isaiah, then political and social action are futile. The only thing left to do is to wait for God to transform the world and human nature. Once metastatic dreams gain the force of society, once they are prevalent in the imaginations of a significant portion of a society, they are difficult to purge. The restoration of order in such circumstances of disorder requires the recognition that "the order of being is the order in which man participates through his existence while it lasts; and the consciousness of passing, the presence of death in life, is the great corrective for futuristic dreams. . . ." The metastatic dream or vision must be broken by individuals who can oppose to it the vision of reality that emerges from the attunement of the soul to the divine. Herein lies the core of the problem of order and history: "the order of society in history is reconstituted . . . through the men who challenge the disorder of the surrounding society with the order they experience as living in themselves" (*OH I*, 536). This dimension of the problem of order was a concern for Christian leaders like St. Paul and St. Augustine. As Voegelin illustrates the point, "The Prophets had to make it clear that the political success of Israel was no substitute for a life in obedience to divine instruction; the Christian statesmen had to make it clear that faith in Christ was no substitute for organized government. . . . The Prophets had to explain that social success was not a proof of righteousness before God; the Christian thinkers had to explain that the Gospel was no social gospel, redemption no social remedy, and Christianity in general no insurance for individual or collective prosperity" (*OH I*, 227).

Volume II: The World of the Polis

Voegelin's analysis of order and history moves from the empires of the ancient Near East and the emergence of revelation in Israel in volume one to the Hellenic polis and the transformation from myth to philosophy in volumes two (*The World of the Polis*) and three (*Plato and Aristotle*). In the empires of the ancient Near East the meaning of existence was symbolized in the language of the cosmological myth. From this compact understanding of reality emerged the more differentiated understanding of reality understood as revelation. The differentiation of revelation is intimately connected to the emergence of historical consciousness in Israel. In the Hellenic polis a parallel differentiation occurs when philosophy breaks with the more compact understanding of reality symbolized in the cosmological myth. Voegelin points out that the shift from Israel to Hellas is not a move forward in time or a superior understanding of truth. He explains that "the Hellenic experience of God as the unseen measure of man is neither a sequel to the Israelite experience of the God who reveals himself from the thornbush to Moses and from Sinai to his people, nor even an intelligible advance beyond it in the sense in which both of these experiences differentiate a new truth about the order of being beyond the compact truth of the myth" (*OH II*, 67). The leaps in being that result in the differentiation of revelation and philosophy occur at about the same time in the Near East and Aegean civilizations. They both transcend the cosmological form but they are independent of one another, and they "differ so profoundly in content that they become articulate in the two different symbolisms of Revelation and Philosophy" (*OH II*, 67).

The historical significance of Hellas is seen in its articulation of the symbolic form of philosophy. The development of philosophy in Hellas has an elaborate genealogy, running through thinkers like Homer, Hesiod, Xenophanes, Solon, Parmenides, Heraclitus, Aeschylus, and Thucydides. The differentiation of philosophy remains latent in these antecedent thinkers, but it explodes in the works of Plato and Aristotle. "The discovery of the soul," Voegelin explains, "as well as the struggle for its order . . . is a process that extends through centuries and passes through more than one phase until it reaches its climax in the soul of Socrates and his impact on Plato." As a consequence, "the Age of Myth is closed" for "[a]fter Socrates, no myth is possible" (*OH III*, 187). This belief explains why Voegelin devoted a separate volume to Plato and Aristotle. Much of the content of *The World of the Polis* traces the development of philosophy in Hellas by way of analysis of the representative thinkers who contributed to the differentiation of philosophy. The compact myth is replaced by the radical transcendence of the divine *realissimum* (the highest reality; the divine ground). Voegelin points out that "the order of the concrete societies, of the polis institutions and their polytheistic cult symbolisms, was not formed by philosophy; and the paradigms of true order developed in the works of Plato and Aristotle never formed the institutional order of any concrete polis" (*OH II*, 94–95). Like the ordering experiences of Israel the experiences of order in Hellas "became ordering forces on a world-historic scale" (95). Philosophy, for example, is what Voegelin calls a "living force" in the contemporary world. In other words, the ordering effect of symbolic forms like philosophy and history have their greatest political and social effect beyond the immediate historical circumstances in which they are created.

Voegelin's analysis of the Hellenistic order is shaped by his insight that whether the topic is Homer's *Iliad* or Plato's *Republic* the primary issue in question is the etiology of disorder and the restoration of order. Homer, for example, was searching for truth about the source of evil. As Voegelin crystallizes the point in his discussion of the *Odyssey*, "What really is at stake . . . is not a progress of morality or theology but the genuinely theoretical issue of the nature of being as far as order and disorder of human existence in society are concerned" (*OH II*, 170). Voegelin is himself searching for primary experiences of the order of being. These experiences are, he believes, the illuminating factors that make the truth about the order of being known. Equipped with the knowledge of order, the philosopher, poet, or prophet is in a position to compare the order of his society to the order that he discovers in his soul, which has been moved by the experiences of transcendence. Homer penetrates to the core of the etiological problem: social and political disorder are caused by the disorder of the soul. While Homer lacks the deeper understanding of Plato and Aristotle, he is aware that there is a part of the human soul that is oriented toward the one, the good, the universal. The ability to perceive life as it is depends on existential openness in this sense. According to Voegelin, Homer was groping toward the idea of the psyche as the sensorium of transcendence.

> Without having a term for it, he envisaged man as having a psyche with an internal organization through a center of passion and a second center of ordering and judging knowledge. He understood the tension between the two centers, as well as the tricks which passion plays on better knowledge. And he strove valiantly for the insight that ordering action is action in conformance with transcendent, divine order, while disruptive action is a fall from the divine order into the specifically human disorder. We can discern the dim outlines of the Platonic anthropology, and even of the Platonic postulate that God rather than the disorderly velleities of man should be the measure of human action. (*OH II*, 177)

Homer and Hesiod are pushing toward the differentiation of philosophy that replaces the myth as the symbolic form in Hellas. The leap in being is not made by Homer and Hesiod, however, because the transcendent-divine source of order is not differentiated by them. Voegelin explains that Homer and especially Hesiod "loosened up" the myth and made it "transparent toward transcendent order" (*OH II*, 195). In this sense Homer and Hesiod are transitional figures in the movement from compactness to differentiation in Hellas. At the level of experience Hesiod and Homer have in a sense made an experiential leap, but they do not make the corresponding symbolic leap in the sense of articulating a deeper understanding and more precise explanation of truth, one that surpasses the cosmological myth. Until the discovery of the transcendent-divine source of order reaches the point of symbolic articulation, the advance to a deeper understanding of truth has not met the threshold of differentiation. This does not detract from the accomplishments of Homer and Hesiod but rather indicates that their contribution to history in Voegelin's sense is as transitional figures rather than as symbolic differentiators.

Nonetheless, the insights of such transitional figures are instrumental to the eventual differentiation that occurs. Plato builds on what Homer and Hesiod discover. Furthermore, Homer, Hesiod, Plato, and Aristotle are all inspired by the spiritual and political disorder of their society. Disorder engenders the quest for order. In the case of Hesiod, Voegelin speculates that "it was the personal distress of Hesiod, his suffering from injustice, that motivated him to break the older anonymity, to appear as the individual man in opposition to the accepted order, and to pit his knowledge of truth against the untruth of society" (*OH II*, 199). Voegelin claims that a connection exists between Hesiod and the Israelite prophets that accounts for the ability of Christianity to penetrate and form a Mediterranean civilization. The Hellenic and Hebrew experiences are parallel in that they deal with the same problem of order, and "[t]he parallel symbols are due to the parallel genius in apperceiving the empirical phenomena of evil" (*OH II*, 231). This "parallel genius" arises from their common experience of social disorder, the anxiety of the soul that it engenders, and the discovery that social disorder has existential roots. Hesiod faces the problem that to survive in a corrupt society he must become unrighteous. This experience moves him toward the differentiation of the soul as the source of order in opposition to the disorder of society, but the "primary being is still the order of social and cosmic reality of which man is no more than a subordinate part" (*OH II*, 227). For Hesiod, "The soul is still inextricably interwoven with the fabric of social and cosmic order; when the order becomes unrighteous, the soul must become unrighteous too, because life has no meaning beyond life within the order" (*OH II*, 226). Voegelin explains: "Hesiod has experienced the anxiety of existential disorder and has discovered its connection with the order of society, as have the prophets; and for the expression of his experience he has developed closely parallel symbols. If Hellenism and Christianity could blend into a common Mediterranean civilization, it was due to the parallel rhythm of spiritual development of Hellas and Israel; and in the beat of this rhythm Hesiod keeps time with the prophets" (*OH II*, 225).

Volume III: Plato and Aristotle

Volume three of *Order and History, Plato and Aristotle,* is a continuation of the search for order in the polis that Voegelin began in volume two. The development of order in Hellas culminates in the differentiation of philosophy; a new symbolic form is created that represents a deeper understanding of human nature and a deeper penetration into the structure of reality.

The philosophical insights of Plato and Aristotle are dependent on the insights provided by the thinkers discussed by Voegelin in *The World of the Polis*. In fact, *The World of the Polis* not only focuses on the connections between the pre-Socratic thinkers and Plato and Aristotle's political philosophy, it also anticipates the breakthrough of philosophy. The story of order in the polis, in other words, is incomplete without the differentiation of the unseen God in radical transcendence as the source of order. Moreover, the psyche is understood as the sensorium of transcendence, the ability of man to sense the pull of the divine toward the *realissimum*. In this sense, then, *Plato and Aristotle* completes the story of the search for order in ancient Hellas. Plato's philosophy of order, his etiology, shapes Voegelin's philosophy of order and history more than any other thinker, including Aristotle.

Voegelin notes that Plato rejects a life of public service even though it is the natural calling for someone in his social position. He chooses instead the life of philosophy because he "understood that participation in the politics of Athens was senseless if the purpose of politics was the establishment of a just order" (*OH III*, 59). Plato, like Socrates, Thucydides, and others, recognizes that the level of spiritual corruption in Athens is too advanced to make politics an efficacious prescription. Through the experience of Socrates, Plato recognizes that "[p]ower and spirit had separated in the polis so far that reunion through ordinary means of political action had become impossible" (*OH III*, 62). Voegelin's characterization of the situation in Athens is bleak: "The order of Athens was not regenerated either by Socrates or Plato. Socrates had to die in the attempt. And Dike [justice] achieved no victory" (*OH III*, 66). The drama of the disintegration of Athenian order is captured by Voegelin in his comments about the setting for the *Theaetetus*. The younger generation of Athens is returning home from battle. Theaetetus is "dying from the wounds received in battle for a polis which rejects his soul but uses his body in defense like a piece of inorganic matter." Voegelin notes that this social condition illustrates "the cold rage of Plato who is compelled to live in obedience to a government of the beast which makes the best die by the beast and for the beast" (*OH III*, 197).

Voegelin's assessment of the Western crisis and his prescription for the recovery of order follows, to a large extent, Plato's philosophy of order. For order to be renewed it is necessary to recover the experiences of order that can, if they achieve social vitality, slowly reorient the souls of individuals. This is what Voegelin calls "the divine, regenerative force of order," which must be made a living force in society (*OH III*, 61). Thus, the problem of order is first and foremost a problem of human consciousness and ethical will, not a problem of politics. Political reform is secondary and predicated on the existence of rulers whose souls have been opened and ordered by the power of the quest for the divine ground of being. This is not to say that the situation in Athens was hopeless. Plato's effort to restore order to Athens includes his belief that "[e]ven the most stubborn politician or sophist, who in public will not listen to the philosopher, still is man and can be stirred up in private. The hard shell of his corruption can be pierced and the anxiety of existence can be touched." Moreover, Socrates does not die in vain. From his death rises the force of Thanatos, "the force that orders the soul of the living, for it makes them desirous of stripping themselves of everything that is not noble and just. . . . Thanatos becomes the cathartic power that cures the soul of the sickness of the earth" (*OH III*, 66–67). In addition, the Eros of the Socratic soul provides the necessary community-forming substance among the participants in the dialogue for the creation of a new order. But to receive Plato's wisdom it is necessary to turn one's soul toward its ordering power.

The Platonic dialogues provide the foundation for Voegelin's philosophy of order. Voegelin's analysis of the *Gorgias* and the *Republic* include characterizations of disorder that can easily be seen as descriptions of the contemporary West, a connection Voegelin makes explicit when he writes, for example, in a discussion of the confrontation and tension between Callicles and Socrates, that "[t]he situation is fascinating for those among us who find ourselves in the Platonic position and who recognize in the men with whom we associate today the intellectual pimps for power who will connive in our murder tomorrow" (*OH III*, 91). Indeed, both Plato's and Voegelin's resistance to disorder have revolutionary implications. In the context of his analysis of Plato's *Gorgias*, Voegelin indicates that the legitimacy of Athens is in question and that corrupt political leaders like Callicles are responsible. If Socrates is correct in his assessment of the situation, then the regime has lost its moral authority to rule; the people can reconsider their loyalty to the current leadership. As Voegelin succinctly states, "The existence of the society in history is at stake" (*OH III*, 82). The hope for a restoration of order depends on the ability of the philosopher to reach the consciousness of others at the level of pathos. At this level of common experience the philosopher has a chance to turn the soul of corrupt individuals toward the good, as long as those individuals are at least to some degree open to the truth of philosophy: "Behind the hardened, intellectually supported attitudes which separate men, lie the *pathemata* which bind men together. However false and grotesque the intellectual position may be, the pathos at the core has the truth of an immediate experience. If one can penetrate to this core and reawaken in a man the awareness of his *conditio humana*, communication in the existential sense becomes possible" (*OH III*, 83–84). The belief that hardened souls can be reached at the level of pathos is one of the reasons why Voegelin's prescriptive response to the Western crisis is to recover the *experiences* of order and transcendence. At the level of experience there remains an awareness of reality that is more difficult to ignore than truth contained in propositions or dogma. To move souls toward the Agathon, the philosopher must confront disordered souls in a way that disables their unwillingness to engage in the search for transcendent reality (logophobia) and cultivates a willingness to seek order and truth.

But what of souls that cannot be reached, as is the case with Callicles in the *Gorgias*? What if the political and social leaders resist conversion even at the level of pathos? Do such conditions warrant political or physical resistance? Is political revolution in order? In the Voegelinian framework the answer is the same as it was for Plato: No. For the philosopher, resistance to disorder must be spiritual, not political or physical. The philosopher must bring to light moral and political corruption. And if the "community of mankind" cannot be restored in history, then it will be in the afterlife where justice is rewarded and injustice punished. "The incrustation of the evildoer that remains impenetrable to the human appeal will fall off in death and leave the soul naked before the eternal judge. The order that has been broken in life will be restored in afterlife" (*OH III*, 84). Once again one might be left with the impression that Voegelin considers politics, under some conditions, rather hopeless.[6] Socrates, Plato, and Aristotle do not and cannot save Athens. Yet it is worth emphasizing that their resistance to Athenian disorder is not in vain. While Athens may be lost, the "authoritative order is transferred" to Plato, who preserves the experience of order in Athens for future generations and societies. "[T]he order represented by Plato has survived Athens and is still one of the most important ingredients in the order of the soul of those men who have not renounced the traditions of Western civilization" (*OH III*, 92).

Not only does Platonic philosophy not save Athens, but it condemns it for its trial and execution of Socrates. Voegelin's characterization of the conclusion of the *Gorgias* is telling with respect to his philosophy of order and history:

> Plato's revolution is a radical call for spiritual regeneration. The people of Athens has lost its soul. The representative of Athenian democracy, Callicles, is existentially disordered; the great men of Athenian history are the corruptors of their country; the law courts of Athens can kill a man physically but their sentence has no moral authority of punishment. The fundamental *raison d'être* of a people, that it goes its way through history in partnership with God, has

> disappeared; there is no reason why Athens should exist, considering what she is. The *Gorgias* is the death sentence over Athens. (*OH III*, 93)

The political and social consequences of the differentiation of philosophy depend on the willingness of society to live in accordance with the truth articulated by the philosopher. Plato's *Republic*, like the *Gorgias*, is written in the context of a society whose younger generation searches in vain for right order. The younger generation has difficulty forming the right order of its soul because of the absence of *spoudaioi* (mature men). The hope for Athens is to recognize Socrates as its savior. But Athens rejects the wisdom of philosophy and thus forfeits its historical existence. That is, Athens continues to exist as a concrete physical entity but it has ceased to exist on the level of spiritual attunement.

One of Plato's primary insights in the *Republic* is what Voegelin calls the "anthropological principle," the idea that the polis is man written large. This fundamental insight has implications for political order. It means that institutions are of secondary importance to the character of the rulers, and a good society can only exist if the rulers who set the tone in society have rightly ordered souls. Voegelin addresses this point when he characterizes Plato's view as being that "legislative matters [like civil, commercial, and criminal law] will take care of themselves if only the souls of the legislating rulers are in good order"

(*OH III*, 141). This order is not created by institutional arrangements but by "the psyche of the founder or ruler who will stamp the pattern of his soul on institutions" (*OH III*, 141). While the order of the rulers' souls is the primary ordering force in society, the order of the philosophers' souls can have only limited political and social influence. Rather, the philosopher's role is to provide a paradigm of right order for the Academy. This conclusion suggests that both philosophy and the philosopher are morally compromised by participating in politics. The deepest order of the soul, Voegelin indicates, following Plato, requires distance from politics. And in Voegelin's mind, Plato's delimitation of politics prefigures Augustine's notion of the city of God (*OH III*, 146).

Aristotle

Voegelin's section on Aristotle in volume three of *Order in History*, like the section on Plato, is a combination of exposition, exegesis, and analysis, but it is not nearly as extensive, nor is it as sympathetic, as Voegelin's analysis of Plato. Voegelin devotes roughly half the space to Aristotle as he does to Plato, and he rates Plato as a better empiricist and superior thinker. He finds that parts of Aristotle's speculation "end in a serious impasse" because his immanentist metaphysics penetrates to the religious dimension of *nous* but does not "recognize the formation of the human soul through grace" (*OH III*, 419). Aristotle's political philosophy prefigures the Christian differentiation of the temporal and spiritual realms, and Aristotle recognizes the divine presence in the soul, but he does not discover transcendent fulfillment as an event outside of history. For Aristotle, the fulfillment of human nature remains part of immanent existence. Voegelin believes that Aristotle is "missing the experience of faith, the *fides caritate formata* in the Thomistic sense." Indeed, "Friendship between God and man is impossible." "The Aristotelian position does not allow for a *forma supranaturalis*, for the heightening of the immanent nature of man through the supernaturally forming love of God." The Aristotelian gods do not "reach into the soul and form it toward its destiny." Aristotle's view, writes Voegelin, is that "human nature finds its fulfillment immanently. Transcendence does not transform the soul in such a manner that it will find fulfillment in transfiguration through Grace in death" (*OH III*, 419–420). Plato comes much closer to the Christian differentiation. Yet, as Voegelin's analysis makes clear, Aristotle is an important thinker in the history of order. As was the case with Plato, Aristotle's political philosophy displays historical consciousness. For Aristotle, the problem of order is not confined to Athens or a particular society. The search for order and the discovery of transcendent reality that it engenders is relevant for all mankind. In fact, Aristotle's political science "is inseparable from a philosophy of historical existence" (*OH III*, 356). Yet

Voegelin also notes that "[t]he order of society in history is theoretically irrelevant to Aristotle because he is convinced that perfect order can be realized within history; the order of history itself becomes of absorbing interest only when perfection is recognized as a symbol of eschatological fulfillment beyond history" (*OH III*, 390).

Aristotle argued that political and social order depended on having a predominance of leaders with ordered souls, not on the balancing of competing individual or class interests. Thus, his political philosophy borrows from Plato the anthropological principle. When the ruling class of ordered souls (*spoudaioi*) is not setting the tone in society, disorder ensues. Aristotle did not believe that Athens had a sufficient number of such *spoudaioi* to realize the best polis. Consequently, while Aristotle believed that perfect order could be realized in history, he did not believe that the realization of perfect order was possible in Athens. Voegelin argues that this assessment of Athenian order moved Aristotle in the direction of considering "new spiritual communities beyond the historical polis of the time" but that he never reaches the point of differentiation because his theoretical horizon was limited by the boundaries of the polis (*OH III*, 410). Aristotle was keenly aware of the particular historical, political, and cultural constraints that give order its ethical quality. The appropriate constitution for a given society is not, then, for Aristotle an abstract question. The answer is contingent on the particular societal ethos. The best regime is not discovered once and for all but requires a repeated search for the appropriate and prudent fit between political form and social conditions. Aristotle understands just how precarious is the order of the good society. Moreover, he realizes that order is formed by a way of life and not by the transmission of information. Politics is about soulcraft, and the *bios theoretikos* and *spoudaios* are the rare individuals who have to varying degrees achieved order in their souls and are thus instrumental to the formation of a just political order. They are standards against which to measure political action; they are models on whose emulation justice depends. The outcome of the struggle for order and the resistance to disorder forms the substance of history as well as the civilizational substance of the society in which the life of order is lived.

For Aristotle political order and existential happiness are predicated on the dominance of *nous* in the ethical life. *Nous* is the part of the soul "where man transcends his mere humanity into the divine ground" (*OH III*, 361). This process of orienting the soul to the divine ground is called "immortalizing." Human beings must discover and be governed by the divine element in their souls if politics and life are to be rightly ordered. *Homonoia*, which Aristotle considers essential to the order of the polis, is a community of individuals who have the common order of the *nous*. Voegelin explains that "[t]he specifically human order of society is the order created through the participation of man in the divine *nous*; just order in society will be realized to the degree in which the potentiality of noetic order becomes actualized in the souls of men who live in society. Justice is ultimately founded in *nous* and *philia*" (*OH III*, 375).

CHAPTER SIX

PHILOSOPHY OF CONSCIOUSNESS

VOEGELIN'S POLITICAL PHILOSOPHY became more abstract and less politically concrete as it matured. His early works—the *History of Political Ideas* volumes, and especially *Science, Politics and Gnosticism* and *The New Science of Politics*—are replete with references to politics. By comparison, his later works, like *In Search of Order*, are politically agnostic, apolitical, or even antipolitical.[1] Greater attention is given to discovering the structure of reality and the process that illuminates the philosophical search for truth in human consciousness, while connections between the search for the divine ground and politics are sparse. Considering his tendency to view the transcendent as something beyond the immanent life of politics, this movement in Voegelin's work is not surprising. Few followers of Voegelin's work seem to express disappointment in or even recognize this change in emphasis, but for those interested in political philosophy it is clear that his earlier works are richer and more relevant. Of course, as should by now be evident, even Voegelin's earlier works can be charged with being philosophically abstract. Voegelin tends to conceive of transcendence in a way that makes its application to politics rather awkward and hesitant, a problem that will be taken up at length in the next chapter. For us, then, the question is how Voegelin's philosophy of consciousness is relevant to political and social life.

The Ecumenic Age

With the fourth volume of *Order and History*, Voegelin breaks with the original plan of the series. Both *The Ecumenic Age* and the fifth volume, *In Search of Order*, are directed more at constructing a philosophy of consciousness than a philosophy of order and history. In explaining the purpose of these two volumes at the end of his introduction to *The Ecumenic Age*, Voegelin reemphasizes that the core problem that defines the Western crisis is that symbols of transcendent experience have lost their meaning and must be restored to consciousness. What stands in the way of recovery "is the massive block of accumulated symbols, secondary and tertiary, which eclipses the reality of man's existence in the Metaxy" (*OH IV*, 107). Thus, the final two volumes of *Order and History* attempt to present "the genesis of the ecumenic problem and its complications" (*The Ecumenic Age*) and to "study the contemporary problems which have motivated the search for order in history" (*In Search of Order*; *OH IV*, 107).

The "ecumenic problem," in Voegelin's terminology, is the task of analyzing variegated historical materials and experiences from a range of civilizations with the objective of finding a common meaning. This pluralistic mode of historiography reveals that consciousness unfolds not in a neat, linear manner but in a way that defies human comprehension. Voegelin traces the unfolding of consciousness and discovers its web-like structure, but he concludes that, ultimately, "it is a mystery in [the] process of revelation" (*OH IV*, 51). Thus, Voegelin's study of order and history does not end in a pronouncement about the ultimate meaning of history, but rather right where it begins, with the continuation of the search for order in historical experience that for the philosopher ends only in death.

The Ecumenic Age begins with a description of historiogenesis, Voegelin's term meaning "speculation on the origin and cause of social order" (*OH IV*, 109). Historiogenesis is classified by Voegelin with three other speculative forms: theogony (the origin of the gods), anthropogony (the origin of man), and cosmogony (the origin of the cosmos). Each form of speculation corresponds to a "sector of reality" (the gods, man, cosmos, society) experienced by human beings (thus Voegelin's beginning to volume one of *Order and History*: "God and man, world and society form a primordial community of being"). These four sectors "exaust the possibility of speculation on the origin of being" (*OH IV*, 111). He notes that "Historiogenesis is one of the great constants in the search [for] order from antiquity to the present," as it can be found in the Orient, ancient Israel, and the ecumenic empires of China, India, and Rome. It can be identified too in modern speculation about the origin and end of history. It is "a millennial constant" (117). It has as its primary objective the quest for the ground. Historiogenetic speculation—like theogonic, anthropogonic, and cosmogonic speculation—illuminates the reality of the ground of being through the creation of symbols inspired by experiences. When the symbolism of the quest remains on the level of myth, it is classified as cosmological. Mytho-speculation, "speculation within the medium of the myth," is a combination of mythopoesis (myth-making) and *noesis* (the activity of *nous*) that fits neither into the category of cosmological compactness or noetic differentiation. Noetic differentiation is the movement away from compact consciousness and its corresponding articulation of reality in the form of myth. It marks the birth of philosophy. Mytho-speculation is an intermediate position between the two symbolic forms mythopoesis and *noesis*. Mytho-speculation is speculation on the beginning (creation) and the beyond (transcendent) articulated through myths; it is part of the search for the origins of order. Historiogenesis, then, is confined by cosmological consciousness.

The Ecumenic Age is the period of history from the rise of the Persian Empire to the fall of the Roman Empire and the rise of Byzantine, Islamic, and Western civilizations (*OH IV*, 188).[2] Voegelin describes it as "the period in which a manifold of concrete societies, which formerly existed in autonomously ordered form, were drawn into one political power field through pragmatic expansions from various centers." The period is significant for the rise of the great religions, including not only Christianity but also "the appearances of Confucius and Laotse in China, of Buddha in India, of Zoroaster in Iran, of the Prophets in Israel, of the philosophers in Hellas." The period marks progress toward the differentiation of a universal order of mankind that extends beyond the physical and political boundaries of empire and world. It is a time of remarkable spiritual development that Voegelin describes as "an opening of spiritual and intellectual horizons that raised humanity to a new level of consciousness," a consciousness "of achieving a new truth of human existence" (*PE 1953–1965*, 135–136).

Voegelin actually identifies two ecumenic ages that unfold parallel in time, one in the West and one in the Far East. But the identification of two ecumenic ages does not denote two mankinds with two separate histories. There is "one mankind with one history" and this is indicated "by virtue of participation in the same flux of divine presence" (*OH IV*, 377). The same God reveals himself in the East and West, and the human beings who experience the divine presence in human consciousness respond in the same structure of reality. The common structure of reality that includes the universal nature of man and the universal structure of consciousness places all men in all societies in the human community that Voegelin calls universal mankind. The differences between civilizations, then, are due to differences of symbolic form, the degree of compactness or differentiation they have achieved, and the exigencies of order which are themselves affected by cultural conditions. However, the substance of history is always the process of differentiating consciousness, and the unfolding of this process is history.

Voegelin states that the defining element of the ecumenic age is the differentiation of the truth of existence from the truth of the cosmos. He turns to Plato as an example of a thinker who understood that "the soul discovers the meaning of existence as a movement in reality toward noetic luminosity" (*OH IV*, 246). Noetic consciousness is gained when Plato and Aristotle discover that the divine is present in man's consciousness and that man's consciousness is moved by the divine intellect. This differentiation is a deeper understanding of the process of consciousness than the more compact cosmological insight that the divine is present in the cosmos; in other words, it further illuminates reality and "[w]hen the process of reality becomes luminous, a line of meaning appears in history" (*OH IV*, 253). To say that a line of meaning exists, however, does not mean that the process that illuminates the structure of reality in history ends. It continues. This explains, in part, Voegelin's focus in the final two volumes of *Order and History* on the structure of consciousness. He defines consciousness as "the area of reality where the divine intellect (*nous*) moves the intellect of man (*nous*) to engage in the search of the ground" (*OH IV*, 249). Human beings are in search (*zetesis*) of the divine, and that search is engendered by an attraction or pull (*kinesis*) from the divine. This process has the characteristic of mutual participation that Aristotle calls *metalepsis*. For Voegelin, discovering the process of consciousness that makes reality become luminous requires the philosopher to overcome obstacles, like doctrinalization and pneumopathology, that prevent the open search for reality and make the process opaque.

Voegelin recognizes that there is a temptation to escape from the search for the divine ground. He refers to one type of escape as "concupiscential exodus," which is a search for new worlds. This state of consciousness is evident in the romanticism manifested, for example, in some advocates of space exploration.[3] Voegelin writes that "we live in the age of other worlds than our own, of invasions from Mars, and of flying saucers. Anything will do, as long as it puts off the confrontation with the divine mystery of existence" (*OH IV*, 273). But Voegelin draws on

Anaximander's dictum: "'The origin (*arche*) of things is Apeiron. . . . It is necessary for things to perish into that from which they were born; for they pay one another penalty for their injustice according to the ordinance of Time'" (277–278). Voegelin, always firm in his conviction that the structure of human nature is inescapable and that politics cannot be used to transgress the boundaries of reality, reminds us of the significance of Anaximander's dictum: "If reality is understood in the comprehensive sense of Anaximander's dictum, obviously man can neither conquer reality nor walk out of it, for the Apeiron, the origin of things, is not a thing that could be appropriated or left behind through movements in the realm of things. . . . [N]o exodus from bondage is an exodus from the *condicio humana*; no turning away from the Apeiron, or turning against it, can prevent the return to it through death" (278).

Man's variegated experiences with transcendence reveal that whatever form transcendent experience takes, the God who reveals himself to man is the same God throughout history. Voegelin states that "the God who appeared to the philosophers, and who elicited from Parmenides the exclamation 'Is!,' was the same God who revealed himself to Moses as the 'I am who (or: what) I am,' as the God who is what he is in the concrete theophany to which man responds. When God lets himself be seen, whether in a burning thornbush or in a Promethean fire, he is what he reveals himself to be in the event"

(292–293). Voegelin also notes that revelation is not information "arbitrarily thrown out by some supernatural force, to be carried home as a possession, but the movement of response to an irruption of the divine in the psyche" (296–297). This irruption in the psyche has a structure, and Voegelin's philosophy of consciousness aims to systematically analyze that structure and the part it plays in the discovery of truth in history. Essential to Voegelin is the preservation of the balance of consciousness that is lost when "apocalyptic and Gnostic sectarians" attempt "to find shortcuts to immortality" (302). For example, St. Paul is criticized for not keeping the balance and engendering the "metastatic expectation of the Second Coming" (306).

The final volume of *Order and History* focuses on specific experiences with transcendent reality as a way of demonstrating what they are and how one goes about the task of recovering their ordering force. In one sense, *In Search of Order* demonstrates and makes more explicit what Voegelin had been doing all along in the previous volumes of *Order and History.* It is a meditative exercise, one that attempts to explain in more detail than was evident in the first four volumes how the process of recovering transcendent experience takes shape. The implications of recovery are not spelled out by Voegelin in this final volume, but taken in the context of his previous work on the Western crisis they are clear: Recovering the historical experiences of transcendence is an essential step in the restoration of political and social order in the West.

Structures of Consciousness

Voegelin's philosophy of consciousness attempts to demonstrate that what unfolds in history is the structure of consciousness. Historical experience is an ordering force because it reveals this structure and enables the philosopher to attune his consciousness accordingly. Consciousness is not an object "but the very process in which reality becomes luminous to itself." The process by which reality becomes luminous is not controlled or managed by the philosopher, but he is aware of participating in it. The philosopher is moved or pulled by the divine toward certain dimensions of the quest. "Reality is in flux" (*OH IV*, 279), which means that the discovery of truth is not a matter of searching for a stagnant order but participating in a dynamic order. In a passage that illustrates why Voegelin was so adamantly opposed to dogma, he explains the precarious grip that human consciousness has on a reality that is in flux: "The truth of the process need not emerge, if it were there already; and when it emerges, it is not a possession beyond the process but a light that casts the process in the role of the darkness from which it emerges. What becomes manifest is not a truth on which one can settle down forever after but the tension of light and darkness in the process of reality" (*OH IV*, 280). Voegelin uses Husserl's concept of "intentionality" to refer to the relation between human consciousness and reality. Consciousness, according to Voegelin, is consciousness of reality, that is, consciousness intends reality as its object. Reality becomes luminous in consciousness, which is the event of knowledge. The truth of the experiences of consciousness is expressed through language.

Another important concept to Voegelin's philosophy of consciousness is "reflective distance."[4] While humans come to know reality by participating in it—they cannot escape the metaxy—there is nonetheless a sense in which they are aware of their ignorance. Jürgen Gebhardt explains reflective distance and its place in Voegelin's philosophy of consciousness:

> By introducing the term "reflective distance" Voegelin designates the reflective acts of consciousness and the concomitant reflective symbolization as the authentic area of the philosophical inquiry. Reflective distance bridges the gap between the "absolute" truth experienced by a person and the "relative" truth documenting itself in the historical manifold of human self-expression. Reflective distance brings out the interplay between the philosopher's imaginative attempts at symbolization and the remembering activity of his consciousness that is noetic anamnesis. The language of reflective distance refers analytically to the personal dimension of human existence in terms of the meditative complex of consciousness-reality-language which provides the symbols with their contextual validity; it relates to the social dimension of human existence in terms of a social field of public consciousness which furnishes the mutual understanding of existentially committed hu-

> man beings. And, finally, it is concerned with the historical dimension of human existence in terms of man's search for his humanity and its order which assigns to the symbols their validity in the context of their historical equivalences. (epilogue to *OH V*, 133)

Voegelin credits Aristotle with the discovery of equivalence. Aristotle understood that "[t]wo symbolisms are equivalent in spite of their phenotypical differences, if they refer recognizably to the same structures in reality" (*OH IV*, 248). Equivalence exists when the same truth is articulated in different languages or at different levels of clarity. The expression of truth about reality varies from compactness to differentiation but the reality is the same and is recognizable as being part of the same search for the ground. Whatever symbolic form is used to articulate the search for, and experience with, reality, the equivalence of symbols makes one search recognizable to another. Voegelin even considers those searches for the ground that are deformations of truth equivalent with those that are expressions of truth in myth, revelation, and philosophy. That is, those who resist truth are usually aware of what they are resisting even if they refuse to orient their souls to it.

Reflective Symbols vs. Original Symbols

Original symbols are those that are created by the person who articulates the engendering experience. Reflective symbols are those that are created by the philosopher who imaginatively recreates the engendering experience and creates new symbols to articulate the truth of order. In the process of imaginatively recreating past experiences the philosopher uses *anamnesis* (bringing back into memory experiences that have become dormant in consciousness) to reenact the experiences of the past. And the purpose of recovering the experiences of order is to restore public consciousness of the engendering experiences so that they will have an ordering effect on individuals and society. This objective is the link between Voegelin's philosophy of consciousness and politics. The assumption is that public consciousness has become infused with ideologies that deform the perception of reality. In this state of deformation, reality becomes opaque and the fantasies of ideological dreams—second realities—are substituted for first reality.

Voegelin is aware that the philosopher's representation of truth is not likely to be accepted by a society that is corrupted by ideological deformation and disorder. But the philosopher's story may have its intended ordering effect if those who hear it are existentially open and can recognize in it the same authority that is present in every man's consciousness. Voegelin uses the Heraclitian term *xynon*, or "common," to refer to that part of the human consciousness that is common to all men. The divine presence in human consciousness is what the philosopher is aiming to awaken by his story. If it can be awakened, then the spiritual substance to resist disorder can form and the transformed individual can actively oppose disorder.

There is an important historical element to Voegelin's philosophy of consciousness. The discovery of reality in consciousness, the various differentiations of truth in history, have a fundamental similarity. The quest, for example, has the same basic structure and the object of the quest is always truth of the divine ground. Voegelin uses Plato's concept "parousia" to denote that there is a divine presence in the process of becoming conscious of reality, that human consciousness is guided by the divine presence within it. Because the basic structures and experiences of consciousness are equivalent across time, past discoveries of truth are connected to the present and future search for truth. Voegelin explains that "the presence of the divine as the moving factor in the soul" identifies "the various events which are equivalent and makes them recognizable to each other." We recognize past experience with consciousness of reality and its articulation because "we recognize in it the quest for the same presence." Regardless of the degree of differentiation or compactness, the structure of consciousness includes the experience of the *parousia* and thus gives to historical experiences with divine reality a universal and timeless element.

> One can . . . not say that past events of consciousness and experience belong to the past, or that future events will belong exclusively to the future, because what makes them events as events of consciousness is what I would call the "indelible presence" of the

> divine, which identifies the tension in relation between man and the divine ground. So all past events are present in the sense of the indelible presence, and therefore belong to the same structural problem and the same reality in historical process of compactness and differentiation. And therefore do we have a history; and, you see, a history that is intelligible. What makes the history intelligible is the parousia in all cases.[5]

The common presence of the *parousia* in experience and the articulation of consciousness is what makes history intelligible. And as the search for order in particular societies plays out in the drama of history, the history of mankind becomes luminous. Voegelin, in other words, is not only concerned with the history of order in particular societies. These individual histories are, no doubt, an important part of his attempt to discover the origins and evolution of the Western order. But what the study of the individual societies also indicates is that their parallel features are part of a larger process of history in which the history of mankind is unfolded. Voegelin describes this larger process of history as "the order of mankind beyond the order of society" (*OH I*, 13). The result of distinguishing between two levels of history is that "a group of societies with separate histories can be treated . . . as if they were a single unit in history, and even that the symbols developed to express a concrete order can be abstracted from the society of their origin and attributed to mankind at large" (13–14). The cosmological myth, for example, is "a typical phenomenon in the history of mankind" because although it forms in culturally specific styles it is present in various and culturally unconnected societies. The experiences of order in particular historical societies have relevance for all human beings because they illuminate truth about the same structure of reality in which all humans exist. The differentiation of the structure of reality is what binds humans in history.

CHAPTER SEVEN

VOEGELIN'S CRITICS

As MIGHT BE expected for so original and contrarian a thinker, Voegelin's work has not been without its critics. This chapter will forego a comprehensive review of the criticism Voegelin's work has evoked and instead focus on two major complaints. The first is that Voegelin's understanding of transcendence is insufficient because it tends to be *radically* transcendent, that is, ahistorical and ethically and politically abstract. The abstractness of Voegelin's conception of transcendence, it is charged, emanates from a romantic view of transcendence. Critics charge that this aspect of Voegelin's political philosophy is manifest in his admiration for Plato and Augustine and his hostility toward Hegel. It can also be recognized, to a degree, in Voegelin's criticisms of Cicero and Aristotle,[1] and it can be inferred from his lack of interest in the contrasting political theories of Burke and Rousseau. The second major criticism is that Voegelin's work is insufficiently sympathetic to Christianity. This critique has two related components. First, Voegelin is accused of not embracing Christian beliefs and dogmas. Second, Voegelin is criticized for undervaluing Christianity as a foundation for the restoration of Western social and political order.

David Walsh, who is a proponent of this second line of criticism, also thinks that Voegelin mischaracterizes and unnecessarily depreciates modern political theory, as can be seen in his often polemical treatment of Hegel's philosophy. The charge is that Voegelin draws too stark a contrast between ancient and Christian philosophy on the one hand and liberalism or modern political theory on the other. Walsh, for one, finds a significant continuity between the older tradition of Plato, Aristotle, and the Christians, and modern thinkers like Hobbes, Locke, Rousseau, and Mill. He faults Voegelin for not recognizing this continuity and for failing to acknowledge the spiritual attributes of liberalism.

Walsh's Criticism of Voegelin

David Walsh's *The Growth of the Liberal Soul*, while not explicitly directed at Voegelin, contains arguments that represent a significant disagreement with aspects of Voegelin's work. Moreover, in his introduction to volume three of Voegelin's *History of Political Ideas*, Walsh describes as a weakness of Voegelin's work "the inability to recognize the liberal constitutional tradition as the publicly effective evocation of the philosophic Christian sources of order" (*HPI III*, 21). In Walsh's view, the success of the liberal constitutional tradition in creating political and social order in the West is a result of the influence of Christian experience on liberalism. Voegelin's characterization of modernity and liberalism as gnostic cannot be reconciled with Walsh's argument. Voegelin traces the roots of modern constitutionalism to the medieval world and in doing so makes connections between the tradition of Greek and Christian philosophy and modern constitutionalism. But the liberal political tradition and the tradition of constitutionalism are seen by Voegelin, for the most part, as deformations of Christian philosophy rather than as reconstitutions of it. Walsh attributes this interpretation to Voegelin's "reserved estimate of [liberalism's] achievement and prospects," which Walsh is more than willing to acknowledge. Walsh explains that Voegelin "witnessed the transmutation of the Weimar Republic into the Third Reich," and he adds that Voegelin's failure to see the Christian substance in the liberal tradition "may have arisen from the pronounced lack of philosophical coherence that has given the liberal constitutional tradition the appearance of greater instability than it in fact has" (*HPI III*, 19). Walsh also claims that while Voegelin fails to see the philosophical commonality in the Christian and liberal traditions, he does recognize this commonality in his analysis of Aquinas. But it is one thing to recognize the continuity between

Aquinas and liberal constitutionalism and another to recognize it, as Walsh does, between Aquinas and thinkers like Hobbes, Locke, and Rousseau.

Walsh characterizes the position of Voegelin and Leo Strauss as "escapist."[2] He believes that they draw such a stark contrast between the modern and premodern traditions that reconciliation between the two becomes impossible. As Walsh defines the problem, "A trenchant critique of liberal politics is an indispensable first step, but can the meditation afford to rest there? It is almost as if the critics have given up entirely on the effort to remediate the liberal framework from within and are now confined to recording its inexorable descent into the maelstrom. One is struck by the absence of much serious reflection on how liberal self-understanding might be modified to accommodate the critics' insights. An impression is conveyed of having already abandoned the effort at remediation."[3] Walsh suggests that giving up on the liberal tradition, as Voegelin has, makes it "difficult to resist the conclusion that the discussion has been merely an exercise in longing for an irrevocably vanished past." What is the point, Walsh asks, "of reflecting on the superiority of the premodern traditions if it is not to draw them into this world as a source of order? If that is the intention, then some attention must be given to the question of how capable the liberal ethos is of absorbing such insights and how the insights might be organically promoted within the liberal construction.

A mere assertion of premodern truth, without any attempt to mediate it in language that renders it minimally intelligible from a liberal perspective, would be futile."[4]

Walsh, no doubt, has a point. Merely to criticize the liberal tradition and point to the premodern tradition as superior would be escapist. The issue in assessing Walsh's criticism of Voegelin is whether what Walsh deems consistent with, or a reconstitution of, premodern truths in the liberal tradition is actually compatible with the older tradition. While Voegelin's position may risk separating the premodern and modern traditions too starkly, Walsh's position may have the opposite problem. If, for example, Rousseau's understanding of pity and self-love is, as Walsh claims, "surely not far from the gospel sense of loving others *as* ourselves,"[5] then that liberal anthropology may eclipse the Christian view that one must submit one's passions to a mediating power in the soul. While Voegelin does not address this specific issue and has little to say about Rousseau, it seems clear that Voegelin's Christian view of human nature and Rousseau's are incompatible and irreconcilable. Such is certainly the case with regard to Hobbes. Walsh is correct in stating that Voegelin does not believe that the liberal tradition can be the source for a restoration of order in the West, that it is something to be resisted because it is part of the deformation of order. Ultimately, it appears that Walsh is too sanguine about the spiritual substance of liberalism.

Voegelin and Conservatism

Given Voegelin's treatment of left-wing ideologies it is not surprising that he is criticized from the political and intellectual Left. The political Right, however, has been more attentive to—and has provided more substantive criticism of—Voegelin's work than has the Left.[6] This is because Voegelin's work deals with topics of great interest to conservatives, including transcendence, history, and order. But while conservatives are among Voegelin's greatest admirers, that admiration is not mutual. Voegelin classifies conservatism as an ideology, or what he sometimes calls an "ismic" construction. Specifically, Voegelin considers traditionalism and conservatism to be "secondary ideologies" (*A*, 189). By this term he means that traditionalism and conservatism were created as a response to radical and revolutionary ideologies. For example, Friedrich Hayek became a conservative because classical liberal ideas were under attack from radical and revolutionary movements like communism.[7] The purpose of conservative and traditional ideologies is, then, to contain and retrench the political, social, and intellectual progress of radical and revolutionary ideologies in order to preserve the wisdom of the past embodied in conventions such as law, custom, and religion.[8]

Voegelin rejects the idea that the truth of existence can be adequately represented in tradition divorced from philosophy. While he is not explicit about the point, he leaves open the possibility that tradition can preserve the truth of existence if it is nurtured and reinforced by philosophy. It seems that in a society where common sense and philosophical openness thrive, tradition can contribute to a just order. Once tradition loses its philosophical moorings, however, its principles and doctrines separate from the engendering experiences that gave them life and meaning. As a result of this separation tradition is emptied of its philosophical and experiential substance. The primary experience and its corresponding original truth give way to the shell of tradition, as if tradition represents the truth of existence rather than being the carrier and derivative of the truth. The usefulness of conservatism and traditionalism is undermined by the fact that they tend to be most prevalent when philosophical openness is waning. Burke's defense of tradition, for example, arose in the context of the Jacobins' revolutionary destruction of the conventional order.

Voegelin was particularly concerned about the degeneration of conservatism into ideological closure and spiritual estrangement. For Voegelin, conservatism is the prelude to ideology because it conditions a society to accept doctrinized truth uncritically and unphilosophically. But separated from its engendering experience and unsupported by philosophy, tradition loses its social vitality and becomes one among many competing conceptions of reality. It eventually gives way to ideological doctrines that are antiphilosophical. In short, the "skeptical suspension" of conservatism (i.e., the suspension of the open search for the transcendent ground) often degenerates into outright revolt against the constitution of being. Voegelin rejects conservatism and traditionalism because he is unwilling to concede any philosophical ground that might eventually be arrogated by immanentizing ideologies.

Further evidence that Voegelin was against doctrinalization but not against tradition per se is the fact that he admired the classical and Christian tradition of political philosophy as well as the American and British constitutional tradition. His political writings enthusiastically embrace Western constitutionalism and the Western political heritage more generally. When faced with the task of analyzing concrete political circumstances in the contemporary world, Voegelin did not hesitate to invoke tradition. But when he did, it was with the understanding that by tradition he did not mean a set of philosophically abstract principles or dogmas, but a historical and social prejudice that was philosophically grounded.

Voegelin's acceptance of philosophically grounded tradition is illustrated by a passage from *The New Science of Politics* in which he defends the classical and Christian tradition of political theory. He remarks, "[W]e may arrive in the course of our endeavors at the theory that the justice of human order depends on its participation in the Platonic Agathon, or the Aristotelian Nous, or the Stoic Logos, or the Thomistic *ratio aeterna*.

For one reason or another, none of these theories may satisfy us completely; but we know that we are in search for an answer of this type" (*NSP*, 6). That is, what matters to Voegelin is not so much the specific content of the answer but the philosophical thrust of the category of answers that he lists. The insights of Plato, Aristotle, the Stoics, and Aquinas constitute a tradition that embodies philosophical truth. Voegelin considers his work part of this tradition, but he wants to avoid the impression that it somehow represents an end to philosophical searching. Past philosophical insights are but a starting point. Moreover, good tradition avoids philosophical stagnation and reification; it is part of an ongoing process of discovering, rediscovering, and differentiating the truth of existence. Tradition, in this sense, provides direction to philosophical search but is not the end of the search.

In light of Voegelin's openness to philosophical tradition it may be that he uses the term "conservatism" in so narrow a way that its meaning precludes what might be called nonideological conservatism.[9] He cites Protagoras the Greek sophist as the first conservative and links moral skepticism and conservative adherence to law and custom to the "simple conservatism" of Pyrrho and Sextus Empiricus.[10] What Voegelin means by this is that Protagoras was skeptical or agnostic regarding the reality of transcendence but conservative regarding historical order. This attitude is characterized by a "skeptical suspense" of philosophical questions that pertain to the transcendent ground of existence. Voegelin includes in this category of conservative Montaigne, Bayle, and Hume. Their "hybrid position" is ultimately flawed because it denies the ability of man to know the reality of transcendence that is the very substance of order that the conservative wishes to preserve. Voegelin says of Hume, "He is a conservative, swimming along in a settled society; he has no principles except the desire of maintaining the pleasant state of things without disturbance. He is a conservative, but he is intelligent and acknowledges that his sympathy for, and enjoyment of, the existing order is equivalent to an absence of principles. . ." (*HPI VII*, 158).

The theoretical flaw of conservatism is exposed when the "archaic wisdom in the conservative mind" is posited as the foundation for order in response to conditions of revolutionary ideological change. Under such conditions the conservative will assert the truth of archaic wisdom that has been reified into dogma or tradition as the solution to the disorder caused by revolutionary ideological movements. Teaching and institutionalizing reified dogmas in a society that is losing touch with those dogmas becomes the social project of conservatism (*OH II*, 382–383). Historical and philosophical truth is codified into traditions and propositions, like natural law, that are then available to use as ideological and political countermeasures against the dogmas of the radical and revolutionary ideologies. But the proper response to the revolutionary and radical, Voegelin submits, is not right doctrine but the rightly ordered soul.

The perplexing and enigmatic relationship between Voegelin's political theory and conservatism is better understood if his critique is applied to a thinker like Burke. Although Voegelin had little to say about Burke, his political writings in particular contain elements of Burkean conservatism. Like Burke, Voegelin is reacting to revolutionary movements that are disrupting the foundation of Western political order. Both men identify the core of modern revolutionary movements to be a pseudo-spirituality that rejects genuine transcendence. They both hold sober and realistic views of human nature and politics that are grounded in historical experience. Burke, then, is an example of a conservative thinker who defended tradition as a way to protect the wisdom of the ages. But Voegelin's virtual silence on Burke makes evaluating their theoretical compatibility difficult. In the eight volumes of the *History of Political Ideas*, for example, Burke is mentioned once, and only then in a passing reference. Furthermore, Burke's conservatism does not fit neatly, if at all, into Voegelin's characterization of conservative skepticism. Either Voegelin remains open to the possibility of another type of conservatism or he discounts the possibility of a type of conservatism that is sufficiently grounded in transcendent reality. The latter seems to be the case. If so, it would explain why some Voegelinians—and even Voegelin himself—

seem to be puzzled by the attraction that his work had and continues to have among many political and intellectual conservatives.

Voegelin's characterization of conservatism as a secondary ideology suggests that it is inconsistent with his political philosophy. But the thrust of traditional conservatism—as illustrated in the work of Russell Kirk, for example—is its desire to restore the truth of transcendent reality in a nonideological way, something that was at the core of Voegelin's work.[11] Voegelin's political theory is, however, clearly at odds with some aspects of Burkean conservatism. In particular, Voegelin seems to reject the idea of value-centered historicism, a position that is implicit in Burke's political theory. Value-centered historicism considers the universal as intimately bound up with particular historical experience.[12] But Voegelin tends to radically separate the one from the many. History never measures up to the universal, for Voegelin, which can be seen in his hesitation to consider transcendence in its concrete historical manifestations and his adamant rejection of all ismic constructions. Voegelin recognizes the participation of both the human and the divine in consciousness but shies away from it when analyzing politics. He tends to avoid concrete representations of transcendence largely because he is so adamantly opposed to doctrinalization. That Voegelin considers the political theory of some conservatives to be insufficiently grounded in transcendent reality parallels the criticism of some conservatives that Voegelin tends, like Plato and Augustine, to conceive of the transcendent abstractly, as something distant from the concrete world of politics.[13] In this regard there is an important difference between Burkean conservatism and Voegelin's political philosophy.[14]

Voegelin's Understanding of Transcendence as Abstract

The effort to reestablish, in political theory, transcendent reality as the moral foundation for political and social order is one of Voegelin's principal contributions to political science. Thus, it is not surprising that Voegelin's thought is disparaged by those representatives of academe and elite culture who consider a transcendence-based political philosophy to be archaic. Because Voegelin was such an ardent proponent of a universal moral order, few who are sympathetic to his efforts have questioned or bothered to carefully examine his understanding of transcendence. The intellectual and cultural debate has tended to be about whether or not there *is* a transcendent reality, not about the *nature* of transcendent reality. But as the recovery of symbols and experiences with transcendent reality has progressed—and there has been progress—more attention is being given to the meaning of transcendence and its place in the philosophy of politics.[15] In this new climate Voegelin's understanding of transcendence has not escaped scrutiny. He has been criticized for developing an understanding of transcendence that is ahistorical and thus abstract. His understanding of transcendence conceives of universality as so radically transcendent that it tends to the opposite extreme of modern philosophy. Modern philosophy radically immanentizes the transcendent. Voegelin overreacts to modern immanentization and radically transcendentalizes the universal. At issue is the relevance of Voegelin's conception of transcendence to political life and order.

Stephen Tonsor remarks in a review of Voegelin's work that "Aristotle is present but does not constitute an essential element in Voegelin's thought." He adds, "But to what extent . . . does the noetic experience [that Voegelin recovers in his work] provide direction in the existential choices one must make in everyday life; to the conundrums which one must face in person, in society, and in history? There has always seemed to me to be a terrible vagueness in Voegelin's possible ethics and politics. It is rich in injunctions as to what it is impossible for humans to achieve; it is less satisfactory as a guide to what we must do." Tonsor's judgment of the relevance of Voegelin's work is severe: "No doubt it is very satisfactory as a contemplative guide for a fourth-century anchorite but is it a satisfactory life-guide for a late-twentieth-century man?"[16]

Clarifying the meaning of Voegelin's understanding of universality is important because the primary focus of his political philosophy is human experience with transcendent reality. Voegelin contends, echoing Plato's anthropological principle, that attunement to the transcendent ground is what engenders existential order and creates social and political order. In short, the transcendent ground is the standard for justice. The criticism is that his use of the concept "transcendent," and his understanding of universality more generally, is abstract to the point that it obscures his political philosophy and may be counterproductive to the cause of reestablishing the transcendent ground of politics.

A representative example from Voegelin's work will help flesh out this critique. Voegelin holds the political theory of Augustine in high regard. He considers Augustine's "formulation of the problem of exodus" as "philosophically perfect" and "extremely beautiful" (*PE 1966–1985*, 105–106). For Augustine, exodus means "to abandon one's entanglements with the world, to abandon the love of self, and turn toward the love of God." Both Voegelin and Augustine believe that the soul is purified by withdrawing from the world. As Voegelin writes, "When the tension is strongest toward the love of God, then we find an exodus from the world" (105). Voegelin clarifies that by exodus he means "a movement of the heart." The new state of existence, the turning away from the world, creates a tension between the existing social and political order and the transformed soul, and this tension often leads to a physical exodus from the existing order. Voegelin cites the exodus of the Israelites from Egypt and the Pilgrims from Holland and England as examples of exodus that have both spiritual and physical aspects.

Voegelin's analysis of exodus raises the question, Why must the transformed soul necessarily be at odds with the world? The world is, no doubt, partly filled with individuals who live according to the love of self (*amor sui*). The good man ought to be at odds with the part of the world that rejects the love of God (*amor Dei*) but at the same time be in community with individuals who share a quality of will that is shaped by moral conscience and the love of God. In one sense Voegelin is right in stating that the ordered soul is at odds with the world and that the resulting tension leads to exodus. Yet he seems to overstate the case. The "movement of the heart" may lead some to follow a deeply spiritual life that takes them away from the affairs of the world and *especially* the life of politics. A figure like Mother Teresa fits this character type. Yet even Mother Teresa was engaged in worldly affairs to some degree. And others who have transformed their character in accordance with the love of God may choose a different path to the good life. They may feel morally compelled to take on the responsibilities of political leadership or some other form of public life. In fact, they are precisely the type of people who should become "entangled with the world." They can enrich civilization and shape politics in a way that inspires others to the good life. They can also confront and counteract those who demean civilization at the immediate level of political power, rather than from the distant aloofness of the soul in exodus. No doubt the good society needs philosophers, poets, and saints to remind us of our higher duties and to create the spiritual capital with which a just order can be built. To do this spiritual and aesthetical work requires a certain distance from politics. Yet politics should not be left merely to those who are inspired by Machiavellian motives. Voegelin, like Augustine, understands this point and yet both have a tendency to depreciate politics to the point that it seems an unworthy vocation. For political life always falls short of philosophical truth.

Voegelin's depreciation of politics is illustrated by his analysis of the Sermon on the Mount.

> [T]he Sermon on the Mount is not a code for life in the "world"; it is addressed to men who live between the worlds in eschatological expectation. In historical existence, entangled in the network of social obligations, man has to pay his debt to nature and is obliged to commit acts in violation of the sermon. If he is struck on the right cheek, he will not turn his left, but hit back in defense of his life, his family and his community. But in hitting back, he will do good, as a Christian, to remember the sermon, and to be aware that in defense he is involved in guilt and that the man who struck him may have had quite as excellent "worldly" reasons for the attack as he has for the defense. Both are involved in a common guilt, both are engulfed in the inscrutable mystery of evil in the world; and in their enmity both have to respect in each other the secret of the heart that is known only to God. (*HPI VIII*, 281)

That violence is at times necessary in political life is due to what Voegelin calls "worldly" reasons. Yet he makes it seem as though any use of violence is somehow a violation of the good and at best a necessary evil. If this is so, then Voegelin's depreciation of politics is justified. But if human nature and political life make violence necessary, why is its use in certain circumstances necessarily evil? Voegelin's view precludes the possibility that violence can be used in accordance with the good. Like Augustine, he tends to denigrate politics because it is directed by worldly concerns. But the world is where we live and search for the good life. The issue here is not that statesmen can somehow avoid earthly responsibilities like providing for common security and economic well-being. The issue is rather that when statesmen do the work of politics they can do it in a way that fosters civilization or in a way that destroys it. In either case violence and other actions that violate the Sermon on the Mount will be necessary. Voegelin and Augustine are realists in that they recognize this, and yet acknowledging the necessities of politics leaves them somewhat disgusted with it. The gap between the city of God and the city of man, the divide between philosophical truth and political necessity, is too great to bridge in this world. Consequently, political life is a disappointment because it fails to measure up to philosophical truth. This disappointment is evident in Voegelin's assessment of Cicero.

Voegelin criticizes Cicero because he is not sufficiently philosophical. In one sense, he may have a point; Cicero is not a technical philosopher. But at the same time Voegelin seems to underestimate Cicero's commitment to ordered liberty and his understanding of law and justice.[17] Cicero's political philosophy can be viewed as more complete than Plato's because it does more to reveal the needs of politics. Statesmen like Cicero and Burke were indeed entangled in the world—and the world is better off because of it. Their sober wisdom may not reach the technical depths of Plato, but their examples as leaders and the practical wisdom embodied in their writings and speeches confront the concrete demands and reality of political life in a way that Plato's political philosophy does not. It is curious that Voegelin admires the Western order that Cicero and Burke helped to forge but at the same time depreciates their contribution to the history of political theory. Voegelin tends to recoil from thinkers who find the universal in particular political life for fear that they immanentize and thus corrupt the transcendent. He thinks men of action are inferior to men of pure contemplation for the same reason. There is a part of Voegelin that did not want philosophy to be contaminated by the life of politics. It is this aspect of Voegelin's political theory that gives it an abstract quality.

The abstractness of Voegelin's understanding of transcendence suggests a degree of moral escapism, insofar as the acceptance of a high moral ideal, as one finds in aspects of Plato's political theory, requires that one remain apart from politics in order to preserve moral dignity. Plato's good man, for example, must be forced to give up the contemplative life to enter political life. The assumption is that the search for truth and virtue is corrupted by politics. Such a view creates in the ethically oriented individual a reluctance to engage in politics. Ironically, taken to an extreme it may create an ethical obligation to avoid the work of creating a just political order. Voegelin was aware of this problem.

On one level Voegelin's political philosophy is very concrete. He did not hesitate to apply philosophical insights to contemporary politics. Note, for example, his comments in *The New Science of Politics* on the failure of the West to contain communism in Eastern Europe: "[T]he Gnostic politicians have put the Soviet army on the Elbe, surrendered China to the Communists, at the same time demilitarized Germany and Japan, and in addition demobilized our own army. The facts are trite, and yet it is perhaps not sufficiently realized that never before in the history of mankind has a world power used a victory deliberately for the purpose of creating a power vacuum to its own disadvantage" (*NSP*, 172). Such comments are common enough in Voegelin's work to indicate that he did not think that as a political philosopher philosophical truths had no relevance to politics. But the issue here is not that Voegelin's work is *politically* abstract, in the sense that he refuses to address concrete issues in contemporary or historical politics. Rather, the question is whether or not his work is *philosophically* abstract—more precisely, *ethically* abstract. If morality is construed ahistorically, then politics is apt to be seen as beneath virtuous individuals. It may be that the historical past is romanticized to contain a model or example of the good society that should be emulated or reconfigured for contemporary times. Yet the contemporary world is likely to reject such historical paradigms, which encourages the conservative romantic to conclude that the contemporary political scene is incapable of realizing the good. Such a view can engender a withdrawal from and a cynicism about politics. At first glance, it may seem strange to think of Voegelin as not being sufficiently realistic about morality and politics. But it could be that (1) the experience with totalitarianism combined with the disintegration of the Western order sufficiently skew Voegelin's view of politics to the point that he does not put much stock in what is possible in politics (in this respect he is a stark realist), and that (2) his philosophical orientation with regard to transcendent reality is somewhat idealistic.

One of Voegelin's critics on the issue of transcendence is Claes G. Ryn. Ryn argues that Voegelin follows Plato's tendency to view transcendence in an ahistorical way. That is, Plato and Voegelin tend to create moral standards for politics that are not sufficiently grounded in concrete historical experience with politics. For example, in the *Republic* Plato has Socrates create a best polis that he admits cannot be realized in the real world of politics. Ryn interprets this to mean that there is an element of moral idealism in Plato's political philosophy (as well as elements of historically grounded moral realism).[18] The imperfections of human nature and human society prevent the ideal from being realized. Plato's description of philosopher-kings and their role in the best polis illustrate Plato's idealism. The American Framers created an elaborate system of checks and balances and constitutional restraints, but Plato's philosopher-kings rule without external restraints on their power. They are capable of using Gyges' ring without abusing it. In the real world of politics such rulers are either nonexistent or do not exist in sufficient numbers for a constitutional order to be based on them. It is not clear that even in the context of fourth-century Athens there was a sufficient number of good rulers to make the city-in-speech (*kallipolis*) possible.

As Ryn notes, critics are likely to defend Plato by arguing, as Voegelin does, that Plato did not intend the best polis as something to be realized and that the *Republic* is not a blueprint for politics. Voegelin is well aware of the criticism that Plato's best polis is an "ideal" or "utopia" and he provides a response to this argument in *The Ecumenic Age*. Voegelin refers to the paradigms of order created by Plato and Aristotle as flawed because they were created "for a society which they knew to be spiritually unreceptive and historically doomed" (*OH IV*, 281). This comment might lead one to believe that Voegelin, like Ryn, finds an element of idealism in Plato's best regime (*kallipolis*). Voegelin, however, claims that the flaw is "seeming only," and that the criticism that Plato is an idealist is a misunderstanding of his philosophy. "The paradigm," writes Voegelin, "is not a construction of social order on the same level as the other types known, only better. Nor is it a utopia or ideal. It is the paradigm of order in the Metaxy, on the new spiritual level achieved in Plato's noetic consciousness" (291). This characteristic separates Plato's *kallipolis* from More's utopia. More's utopia is a construction of an ideal, Plato's best city is not. Yet this reading of Plato's best regime bears out Ryn's point. If Plato's paradigm is not a social or political construction, in what sense is it relevant to political life? If the purpose of constructing the paradigm is to capture Plato's philosophical insights about justice and politics, one would expect that those insights—being derived from concrete political life—can be applied to concrete political life. The whole point of the *Republic* would seem to be that philosophy should inform politics. Yet, there is a sense in which Voegelin and Plato characterize the disorder of Athens in such a way that political resistance to it is futile. The life of philosophy becomes an escape from political responsibility.

Ryn's point is that if the transcendent and its relationship to politics is viewed in a way that recognizes the inescapable connection between universality and history, moral understanding will not be abstract and ahistorical but understood as something that is found in the particular circumstances of historical experience. Politics is what it is and universality must be found within that concrete historical reality, not in some ahistorical ideal. Plato would seem to acknowledge this point when he states that the good man is ready for action (*Republic* 443e). Thus, it is a plausible interpretation that Plato's political philosophy is not, as a whole, idealistic, but there are strains of both idealism and moral realism interspersed through his work. The same might be said for Voegelin.[19]

Voegelin and Christianity

A typical complaint of Voegelin's Christian critics is Tonsor's comment that "Voegelin the 'philosopher' believed in the God of the philosophers and tried again and again, unsuccessfully I believe, to 'put on Christ.'"[20] Tonsor refers to Voegelin's "hostility to doctrinal Christianity."[21] Understanding and evaluating such criticisms requires that Voegelin's work be put in perspective and that a range of critics be considered. Voegelin's Christian critics tend to share with him the desire to restore Western order by reestablishing the truth of transcendent reality. Their disagreement with his treatment of Christianity is due to their favorable view of doctrine and their subordination of Greek philosophy to Christianity in the recovery of order.

Voegelin's primary task is to recover the normative source of order in history: engendering experiences with transcendence. In his view, the disorder of the modern period stems largely from the doctrinalization or reification of transcendent experience into propositions and dogmas, as well as its derailment into ideology. Therefore, the symbols that illuminate the experience of participation with the divine ground of existence have become opaque.

Attempts to recover the meaning of history have failed. The recovery requires an "openness" to the source of meaning, whereas modern attempts at recovery are characterized by Voegelin as "closed." Their closure is defined by the collapse into ideological "systems," "dogma," or "doctrine," such as Hegel's philosophy of history, Marx's economic determinism, or scientific positivism. As was explained in chapter 4, the presuppositions of positivism, for example, exclude transcendent reality from its purview. This is typical of the way in which doctrinal belief inhibits the recovery of engendering experience: it considers the doctrine or method itself as the primary source of truth. Voegelin believes that once existential experience with divine reality is eclipsed by doctrine, the differentiated truths of human existence are in danger of losing their luminosity, a process that is continual. "The doctrinaire theology and metaphysics of the eighteenth century were succeeded by the doctrinaire ideologies of the nineteenth and twentieth centuries; an older type of fundamentalist doctrine was followed by a new fundamentalism" (*PE 1966–1985*, 118).

The primacy of transcendent experience over doctrine is asserted by Voegelin as vital to the recovery of order. Many Christian scholars, however, object to Voegelin's subordination of doctrine to experience. They argue that Christianity represents the ultimate answer to the quest for meaning in history. Moreover, they believe that because it remains somewhat ambiguous about the nature and destiny of man, the philosophical inquiry of Voegelin's study of order and history misses the essential Christian message. It refuses to accept the Christian transformation of history as fulfilled in the Resurrection.

The original scheme for Voegelin's *Order and History* included a volume on *Empire and Christianity* and another volume on *The Protestant Centuries*. The revised scheme eliminated the two volumes on Christianity and reduced the analysis of it to one chapter in *The Ecumenic Age*. Voegelin's Christian readers were disappointed by the elimination of the two volumes on Christianity.[22] But it was Voegelin's interpretation of Christianity's contribution to the meaning of history that they found most troubling. His claim that the "course" of history was ultimately a mystery invited responses like that of Bruce Douglass, who charged Voegelin with underestimating the effect of Christian revelation on the structure of reality. "In place of the biblical image of a God whose presence and purpose in history are made manifest," Douglass states, "we are given a divine flux whose direction is a mystery."[23] Instead of emphasizing Christianity as the fulfillment of history, Voegelin chose to emphasize the imbalancing effects of Christianity on social order: Christianity's eschatological expectation diverted attention away from questions of social and political order and, consequently, Christianity did not provide a civil theology; as a result, the void was filled by gnostic deformations of civil order. Voegelin also stressed Plato's philosophy rather than Christianity as a paradigm of the balance between existential consciousness and social order.

Most of Voegelin's Christian critics consider gnosticism peripheral to the "good news" of the Gospel. Voegelin, they argue, is critical of Christianity for its insufficient attention to temporal order and also its tendency to dogmatize the engendering experience of Christianity, but he seems to ignore the contribution of Christianity as an ordering force on man and society. Gerhart Niemeyer, for example, refers to Voegelin's treatment of Christianity in *The Ecumenic Age* as "deeply disappointing," especially in its concentration on St. Paul as the central figure of Christianity. "Voegelin's exegesis of St. Paul," he points out, "would not have to be changed if one removed Jesus Christ from it altogether." Niemeyer charges that "Voegelin has approached a great spiritual reality from a standpoint extraneous to it."[24] That is, instead of dealing directly with the historical

Christ, Voegelin analyzes St. Paul's vision of the Resurrection and equates it with the historical event itself. The failure to embrace the full range of Christian experience prompted Douglass to characterize Voegelin's attitude toward Christianity as "ambivalent." Harold Weatherby, agreeing with Niemeyer, charges that Voegelin "ignores" the Incarnation and that he misunderstands the implications of Christian doctrine because he is enamored with Greek philosophy. Like Niemeyer, Weatherby complains that Voegelin's treatment of Christianity needs to be more extensive, especially in addressing the core of the Christian message. In exclusively focusing on St. Paul, Voegelin has overemphasized the affinity between gnosticism and Christianity, and has underestimated Christianity's ordering effect.

Douglass is one of the harshest critics of Voegelin's treatment of Christianity. His argument is summarized by his comment that "it would seem to be Voegelin's view that only the discipline of philosophical reason can challenge effectively the modern predicament." Douglass admits that Voegelin recognizes a continuity between Greek philosophy and Christianity but he is unwilling to accept his characterization of Christianity. While Voegelin clearly accepts the Gospel as a representation of "a more complete knowledge of the Unknown God," Douglass complains that "Voegelin recognizes gnostic influences at certain key points in the New Testament, and he argues that *modern* gnosticism bears what would appear to be unmistakable evidence of Christian origins."[25] It is not that Douglass disagrees with Voegelin's assessment so much as he finds his emphasis unwarranted and his prescription misguided. "Voegelin's interpretation of the Gospel," he argues, "leaves something to be desired. What is missing . . . is the sense of the Gospel as salvation."[26] Marion Montgomery makes a similar criticism of Voegelin for giving primacy to Greek philosophy: "For the Christian, as an act of faith, it is the savior and not the poet or prophet or philosopher in whom lies the promise of our return to the lost home. But Voegelin is not prepared to make a surrender through faith to the mediator, though he honors it in others: he sees a danger that, at this point in his quest at least, such a surrender is too near the surrenders to dogma in the medieval world which prepared the grounds in which modern ideologies have flourished."[27] In a footnote to this passage Montgomery criticizes Voegelin for his "severe judgment" on the medieval Church and the scholastics, and he questions Voegelin's assertion that "orthodox dogma and apocalyptic emotionalism in the middle ages . . . prepared the way for Renaissance ideologies." Like Weatherby, he accuses Voegelin of "an aberrational construction of the meaning of the incarnation, one which reduces the event of the incarnation and replaces it with the 'larger' event of the unfolding of humanity."[28]

These criticisms of Voegelin represent not merely a disagreement with his interpretation of Christianity, but a rejection of his philosophical framework. Montgomery in fact finds a "principal dogma at the heart of Voegelin's own work," which he defines as "Thou shalt not rest in conclusion lest thou fall into certitude, the unforgivable sin against openness." The quest for certitude, both Voegelin and Montgomery would agree, is an eternal desire. While the former has developed a theory of consciousness that centers around the belief that what is permanent in the history of mankind is "man in search of his humanity and its order," the latter asserts that "there is a difference between coming to rest in false ground and in truth."[29] Montgomery's criticism is that Voegelin embraces philosophy, not faith, and therefore he must reject all attempts to submit to doctrine or rest in Christian truth. To do otherwise would be to jeopardize the open and critical function of the philosopher. Montgomery implies that Voegelin's thought precludes him from accepting the truth of Christian revelation as a definitive understanding of the human condition. Where Voegelin emphasizes the continuity between philosophy and Christianity, many of his critics emphasize the differences between them.

A more sympathetic analysis of Voegelin and Christianity has come from John H. Hallowell and James L. Wiser. As Wiser states, Voegelin's concern as a philosopher "is to share his experience, not to create a dogmatic system against which heresies can be compared."[30] This experience is not the product of some "methodological technique" but rather of Voegelin's participation in the order of being through his openness to the ground of existence. Openness to the transcendent source of truth is the precondition for the philosopher's participation in the Platonic *methexis* or the Aristotelian *metalepsis*, i.e., the participation and interaction of human and divine will in the search for order. The experience of this participation is described as a "search (*zetesis*) from the side of man and attraction (*kinesis*) from the side of God" (*PE 1966–1985*, 90). It is Aristotle's highest virtue, the practice of immortalizing (*athantizein*). Voegelin explains, however, that "[w]hen the consciousness of existential tension has atrophied—as it has in doctrinal theology and metaphysics of the eighteenth century—we are not thrown back to a pre-Aristotelian belief in mortals and immortals. From the state of confusion, there rather emerges the new type of system which transforms experienced participation in the divine into a speculative possession of the divine" (*PE 1966–1985*, 89).

Wiser acknowledges this point and adds that "existential tension" causes anxiety that individuals attempt to alleviate through gnostic certitude. He also agrees with Voegelin on the failure of Christianity to prevent the rise of gnosticism. "Man's experience of reality," he explains, "may engender this quest for certitude and Christianity's inability to subordinate that quest to the service of the soul's opening towards its divine ground may only be an example of the inevitable failure of dogma when confronting such forces." Thus, while Wiser shares Voegelin's understanding of dogma as an inadequate response to uncertainty, he implies that Voegelin has underestimated the scope of gnosticism. That is, Voegelin implies in his earlier writings that gnosticism is strictly a derailment from Christianity, but Wiser argues that "the tensions within Christianity against which gnosticism reacted are the very tensions of philosophy itself. As such, gnostic closure becomes a single manifestation of a universal human possibility." Voegelin acknowledges gnosticism's pre-Christian roots but Wiser clarifies the point when he explains that "the philodoxic desire for certitude is not simply a rejection of a Christian experience nor even simply a rejection of a philosophical experience. Rather it appears to be a reaction engendered by a fundamental human experience available to all men of sensitivity."[31] The fact that Christianity is the most differentiated understanding of reality accounts for its greater tendency to derail into gnosticism.

Wiser's article implies that Voegelin may have overestimated the ability of philosophy to confront modern gnosticism, especially in light of Voegelin's own admission that "the history of philosophy is in large part the history of its derailment" (*OH III*, 331). In other words, if the modern crisis is characterized as a revolt against transcendence, whether it be the transcendent God of the Bible or the transcendent beyond (*epekeina*) of Greek philosophy, is Voegelin justified in emphasizing philosophy as the most efficacious response to the disorder of the age?

Hallowell's article "Existence in Tension" addresses some of the problems present in answering this question. For one, Voegelin has characterized contemporary Christianity as far removed from the historical drama of revelation. Moreover, Voegelin states that the Unknown God who "was present in the existence of Jesus has been eclipsed by the Revealed God of Christian doctrine." This unfortunate doctrinalization of the essential Christian experience resulted from "the separation of school-theology from mystical or experimental theology. . . ." Voegelin adds,

> Even today . . . when this unfortunate separation is recognized as one of the great causes of the modern spiritual crisis; when energetic attempts are made to cope with the problem through a variety of crisis and existential theologies; and when there is no lack of historical information about either the revelatory process leading up to the epiphany of Christ, or about the loss of experimental reality through doctrinization; the philosophical analysis of the various issues lags far behind our pre-analytical awareness. It will be necessary, therefore, to reflect on the danger that has given the Unknown God a bad name in Christianity and induced certain doctrinal developments as a protective measure, *i.e.*, [*sic*] on the danger of the Gospel movement derailing into Gnosticism. (*PE 1966–1985*, 199–200)

Voegelin goes on to explain in this essay, "The Gospel and Culture," that the Gospel movement failed to clarify the relationship between existential fulfillment in the Kingdom of God and the pragmatic concerns of political and social life. As a result "derailment into Gnosticism became possible." Hallowell responds by commenting that "[i]t is clear that Voegelin considers 'the noetic analysis of the metaxy' in classical philosophy 'in some points superior to anything we find in the Gospel.'"[32] This highlights the point Voegelin makes in *The Ecumenic Age*, where he claims that "Plato kept the theophanic event in balance with the experience of the cosmos. He did not permit enthusiastic expectations to distort the human condition" (*OH IV*, 303). This remark is used as the opening comment on St. Paul. One only needs to read a few pages into the chapter to verify what is implicit in the above passage: Paul did not maintain that balance.

Hallowell protests this characterization of the Gospel. He identifies many unanswered questions in Voegelin's treatment of Christianity. For example, while he accepts that "doctrine divorced from the experience which gave rise to it becomes an empty abstraction and that many doctrinal disputes are much ado about nothing," he inquires, "is *every* attempt to express faith in doctrinal form necessarily doomed to become doctrinaire? And how can existential faith be communicated to others without the aid of doctrine?" While he agrees fundamentally with Voegelin's argument that Christianity has often degenerated into ideology through the reification of doctrine, Hallowell believes that a central component of the Christian experience is missing in Voegelin's work. Questions of the Church or the sacraments are skirted in Voegelin's treatment of Christianity. In addition, Hallowell argues,

> Voegelin seems to be saying that only so long as the Gospel mirrors the tension of existence is it the true Gospel. It is not clear to me what his response would be to those who would say the Gospel is intended to be precisely an answer to this tension, that through the cultivation by the grace of God of the virtues of faith, hope, and charity one might be enabled better to endure the life of tension in the hope that "when the fever of life is over and our work is done, we may be granted a safe lodging and a holy rest, and peace at the last." It is not clear if there is any sense in which Voegelin regards the Gospel as "good news."[33]

A rejoinder to Hallowell's argument is that Voegelin is primarily concerned with building a philosophical foundation on which to support a spiritual revival. He believes that the preliminary task is to recover the meaning of experience. With this as a precondition, Voegelin hopes to restore the primacy of experience to meaningful spiritual conversion. He implies this in "Immortality: Experience and Symbol," when he refers to the state of scholarship at the turn of the century as "a difficult time for men of a philosophical bent." Yet he adds that "since the beginning of the century, the situation has changed substantially." Although Voegelin admits that "the spiritual disease has manifested itself massively in bouts of global war and revolution" he nevertheless believes that "the experiences of transcendence are being recaptured in a peculiarly backward manner." These experiences are being reintroduced as

> "facts of history"—through the exploration of myth, of the Old and New Testament, of apocalyptic and Gnostic movements, through comparative religion, Assyriolgy, Egyptology, classical philosophy, and so forth. This renewed knowledge about experiences on which depends the order in personal and social existence makes itself felt even now in an increasingly accurate diagnosis of the contemporary disorder and its causes; and it would be surprising if it did not become a living force, sooner or later, in the actual restoration of order. (*PE 1966–1985*, 57)

This comment should not be overlooked since it represents a partial answer to Hallowell's important question. Voegelin clearly recognizes two components vital to the recovery of order. The first is the recapturing of the "experiences of transcendence." It is important to note that Voegelin is himself a part of this recapturing, and that in fact he has developed the philosophical framework by which the experiences of transcendence rediscovered in particular fields of study can become a living force in society. The second is dependent upon the first and is referred to by Voegelin as "the actual restoration of order." By this we can assume he means spiritual revival. It is essential to understand that the recovery of "experiences of transcendence" is the precondition to a restoration of "order in personal and social existence."

If the recovery of experience and its rearticulation can be understood as a necessary prerequisite to the "actual restoration of order," then Voegelin's analysis of Christianity should become more acceptable to his Christian critics. Although he does not address certain aspects of Christianity specifically, *Conversations With Eric Voegelin* and "Response to Professor Altizer" contain reflections that help illuminate the issue. For example, Hallowell's question about the communication of existential faith is answered in part by Voegelin's remark that "dogma has a very important social function: to avoid certain misconstructions and show, if the misconstructions are socially dominant, how at least to handle them so as to avoid the worst consequences" (*CEV*, 96). Voegelin's understanding of dogma as being both a necessary protection against misconstructions—that is, symbols that misrepresent the engendering experiences they claim to represent—and having the potential to collapse into reification is also reflected in his "Response to Professor Altizer." He asserts that

> dogma develops as a socially and culturally necessary protection of insights experientially gained against false propositions; its development is secondary to the truth of experience. If its truth is pretended to be autonomous, its validity will come under attack in any situation of social crisis, when alienation becomes a mass phenomenon; the dogma will then be misunderstood as an "opinion" which one can believe or not, and it will be opposed by counter-opinions which dogmatize the experience of alienated existence.

He refers to the problem in the specific historical context in which it developed:

> The development of a nominalist and fideist conception of Christianity is the cultural disaster with its origins in the late Middle Ages that provokes the reaction of alienated existence in the dogmatic form of the ideologies, in the eighteenth and nineteenth centuries. The result is a state of deculturation with which we are all too familiar from our daily talks with students who are caught in the intellectual confusion of a debate that proceeds, not by recourse to experience, but by position and counter-position of opinion. Once truth has degenerated to the level of true doctrine, the return from orthodoxy to "the mystery" is a process that appears to require as many centuries of effort as have gone into the destruction of intellectual and spiritual culture. (*PE 1966–1985*, 295)

Taken in its historical context, Voegelin's position seems to be sensible. For the return to "the mystery" can only come about by a restoration of experience. While Hallowell's queries and reservations are understandable, they must be, in the final analysis, considered as secondary to what Voegelin presents as primary to the recovery of order.

Voegelin is writing at a time in which deculturation has had a significant effect on those who tend to be sympathetic to his philosophy of history but cannot accept his argument against doctrine. Montgomery implies that Voegelin is not existentially willing to accept the full range of Christianity because he "is not prepared to make a surrender through faith to the mediator." Montgomery suggests that what Voegelin means by the statement that "History is Christ written large," is that the Incarnation is one among many differentiations that are all part of "the unfolding of humanity." For Voegelin, the Incarnation does not change the structure of reality but only sharpens our understanding of it. The idea that history has ended as a result of the Resurrection, a position taken by Weatherby, is considered by Voegelin to be fallacious. Weatherby remarks, "If what Christians believe about the Incarnation be true, reality has moved beyond itself, and history is therefore abolished by its very completion. . . . The desire of nations has come; there can be no more desire *in history*."[34] By arguing that the "Incarnation brought history to an end," Weatherby represents precisely the tendency in Christianity that Voegelin criticizes. In declaring the consummation of history, Weatherby's underlying assumption is either that history is something other than man's participation in divine reality or that this participation has been fulfilled. Certainly, taken in the Christian context, history has reached a point of culmination with the Incarnation. Man's ultimate purpose has been revealed as existence beyond time and history. However, the problem of social and political order remains. Man must live and act in a world that demands attention to questions of temporal justice regardless of whether or not Christianity is the final differentiation. While our understanding of man, God, society, and world is further illuminated by Christianity, life in the metaxy continues. Because Voegelin is concerned primarily with order, and not theological speculation, he emphasizes that the anxiety of life in the In-Between is not abolished by differentiation. He explains in the introduction to *The World of the Polis*:

> [H]uman nature is constant in spite of its unfolding, in the history of mankind, from compact to differentiated order: The discernible stages of increasing truth of existence are not caused by "changes in the nature of man" that would disrupt the unity of mankind and dissolve it into a series of different species. The very idea of a history of mankind presupposes that constancy of nature; and the reality of that constancy is attested beyond a doubt by the experiences of the leap in being, by the experience of a transition from untruth to truth of existence in which the same man is the "old man" before, and the "new man" after, he has suffered the infusion of divine Being. (*OH II*, 71)

CONCLUSION

VOEGELIN'S CONTRIBUTION

VOEGELIN'S CONTRIBUTION TO political science and scholarship can be enumerated into seven major components: (1) the restoration of political science via a critique of positivism; (2) a diagnosis of the Western crisis; (3) a critical analysis of totalitarianism and modern ideological movements; (4) recovery of the symbols and engendering experiences of order; (5) a philosophy of history; (6) a philosophy of consciousness; (7) a philosophical framework of openness to transcendence that can be used to restore order to Western civilization. These are the primary components of Voegelin's political philosophy and the result of his life-long devotion to the search for truth and order. They do not constitute an ideology or a set of doctrines, but instead represent the philosophical quest for the ground of being that is the source of resistance to untruth and disorder.

If the measure of a great philosophical mind is mere intellectual capacity, then Voegelin is one among dozens of great modern philosophers. What separates Voegelin from most modern philosophers is not so much a difference of intellect but a difference of imagination. This point becomes clear when Voegelin's imaginative vision is compared to the modern thinkers that he analyzes in his scholarly works. Why is it that Marx, Nietzsche, Heidegger, and a range of other thinkers tend to misconceive the essence of modern life but Voegelin tends to see it as it is? It is Voegelin's imaginative vision. And this vision, like that of other modern philosophers, is shaped by his will. In other words, to see life for what it is requires that the will or soul be oriented to the ground of reality that is the object of philosophical search. Voegelin's conception of reality differs from that of gnostic thinkers like Marx and Nietzsche because his political philosophy represents openness to transcendent reality and their existential disposition is closed to it. Voegelin did not suffer from the pneumopathological and logophobic disposition that he identifies in many modern thinkers. Different character types breed different qualities of imagination. As Voegelin explains: "[W]hat the philosopher moving in the field [of experiences] will see or not see, understand or not understand, or whether he will find his bearings in it at all, depends on the manner in which his own existence has been formed through intellectual discipline in openness toward reality, or deformed by his uncritical acceptance of beliefs which obscure the reality of immediate experience" (*PE 1966–1985*, 116).

Modern philosophy is generally shaped by the gnostic world-immanent imagination, but Voegelin's political philosophy is shaped by the transcendent imagination. It is this difference in imagination, ultimately rooted in a difference of character, that accounts for the contrasting visions of Voegelin and modern gnostics. Voegelin has absorbed in his consciousness the ancient and Christian tradition in a way that shapes his historical imagination and critical judgment. Thus, the modern crisis is ultimately a problem of will and imagination, not intellect. It is not a problem of creating the right political or ideological program but the right conduct, that is, a matter of orienting the will to the Agathon.

The transformation of the will is intimately bound up with the transformation of consciousness. And though the idea of transforming human consciousness has been common in modern political thought, Voegelin differs from most other thinkers who advocate a change in consciousness in that he understands that consciousness cannot be transformed without a parallel and authentic transformation of the soul—what Plato called the *periagoge*. In gnostic ideologies, the Platonic *periagoge* and Christian *metanoia* are replaced by the *libido dominandi* (will to power), and the human will is consequently freed from its transcendent fetters.

Critically judging Voegelin's contribution to political theory and the restoration of Western civilization requires that his arguments be measured against historical experience. Is life—more precisely, the human condition—as he claims? This study has attempted to explain and analyze the central components of Voegelin's political philosophy in a way that allows the reader to evaluate the merits and experiential authority of his work. While critics have identified deficiencies in Voegelin's political theory, on the whole it is a remarkable achievement, one that provides a challenge to the prevailing strains of ideologically driven scholarship and politics. Voegelin's political theory provides a place to gain a theoretical perspective that helps illuminate the nature of the modern crisis and the structure of reality. It can be seen as part of the larger effort in twentieth-century scholarship to restore and reconstitute the classical and Christian tradition in politics and philosophy.

This restoration effort is not an attempt to return to a bygone golden age. Rather, Voegelin has provided an understanding of political, social, and existential order that demonstrates how past historical experiences are the spiritual substance of contemporary order. The engendering experiences of order can be imaginatively reexperienced in a way that shapes human consciousness and prepares it for the specific challenges of contemporary life. The past, then, does not provide a blueprint for human action, but consciousness of historical experience with transcendent reality is the necessary prelude to orienting the soul to the Agathon in changing historical circumstances. Historical experience provides the spiritual substance that illuminates the truth of existence—the truth necessary to order souls and society.

Voegelin's analysis of history and order provides valuable insights on the nature of man, society, and politics. His concept of metastatic faith, for example, originally developed to analyze the prophet Isaiah, also describes contemporary ideologues who believe that, through humanitarianism, politics, and the very structure of reality on which it is based can be transformed. The metastatic imagination is in fact an integral part of modern politics. It is evident in the kind of political and social idealism that issues in the belief that laws and public policies can permanently cure social ills that stem from flaws in human nature. The existential condition that fosters such an imagination is something that Voegelin extensively diagnoses. He provides a prescriptive response to the metastatic personality: sober openness to the reality of the human condition. And he identifies the utopian strain in modern consciousness and critically analyzes its spiritual roots. His philosophy of history and philosophy of consciousness show that behind the morally soothing language of progressive humanitarianism lies the spiritual narcissism that breeds existential, social, and political disorder. The language and superficial embrace of utopian social virtues mask the violence and ugliness that are the fruits of modern ideologies. Voegelin has exposed the spiritual corruption of these ideologies and their ersatz spirituality.

Voegelin's resistance to modern secularism is both historically and philosophically based. One of Voegelin's primary contributions to political science and Western civilization in this regard is his recovery of language symbols that articulate experiences with transcendent reality. In working through an impressive range of historical material and illuminating the meaning of language symbols like myth, revelation, philosophy, and history, Voegelin provides a way for individuals to regain consciousness of transcendent experience. Without consciousness of such experience individuals become estranged from first reality. They either wander aimlessly through life or grip tightly to the ideological doctrines of second reality. In either case the result is the same: the dehumanization of man and the disintegration of civilization. Voegelin's political philosophy is, then, a way of resisting this dehumanizing spiritual estrangement. It is an invitation to intellectually and existentially explore the historical experiences of the past that are the ordering substance of civilization.

Voegelin's contribution also includes his characterization of the Western crisis and his prescriptive response to it. His analysis of the crisis has the advantage of attending to a range of historical materials and philosophical contexts, a broad scope that is missing from most works on the modern world. Moreover, Voegelin has identified the spiritual origins of the Western crisis in a way that creates resistance to it. Modern gnosticism, as defined by Voegelin, is one of the primary characteristics of contemporary politics. Understanding its historical and spiritual roots provides wisdom for discriminating between various spiritual, cultural, and political impulses. It also fosters an ability to distinguish between true and false spirituality. On the other hand, the work of Voegelin's critics makes it evident that his work on transcendence will benefit from a careful examination of universality and its meaning. The abstract tendencies in his conception of transcendence need to be corrected so that the effort to restore the transcendent ground of political theory is not undermined by inauthentic constructions of universality.

Voegelin's greatest contribution may be his resistance to totalitarianism. His work on Marx, the Nazis, and their philosophical predecessors explains how certain strains in the development of political philosophy resulted in mass murder. When politics reaches the point of systematically exterminating tens of millions of innocent human beings, philosophical and historical insights are vitally important to reveal its causes. Not only has Voegelin illuminated the spiritual causes of totalitarianism, but he has done so in a way that demonstrates the connections between totalitarianism and ideologies like liberalism and positivism. The revolt against transcendence and the constitution of being, the "untruth of existence" (*PE 1966–1985*, 49), are the common denominators in all modern efforts to destroy the spiritual fabric of civilization. Critics like David Walsh may legitimately criticize Voegelin for overstating the common intellectual and spiritual roots in totalitarianism and liberalism, but Voegelin's argument seems fundamentally sound.

Without the revival of the Western tradition, there is little chance of cultural restoration. Voegelin has uncovered for us the spiritual experiences of the past that have been largely dormant in Western intellectual and cultural life. The very fact that such historical experiences and the symbols used to articulate them are in need of recovery is an indication that liberalism has not preserved consciousness of the ordering experiences of Western civilization. Consequently, Voegelin had to create a philosophical framework capable of reviving these symbols and experiences. Given that one of Voegelin's objectives was to restore the spiritual substance of the West, his contribution to this effort is impressive. Generations of students and scholars will turn to Voegelin for insights into the nature of order and for the philosophical substance necessary to revive Western civilization. And long after Western civilization has passed, Voegelin's philosophical insights will provide an understanding of the structure of reality that is relevant to anyone who participates in man's search for order.

NOTES

Introduction

1. Voegelin's published and unpublished works are being published jointly by Louisiana State University Press and the University of Missouri Press in thirty-four volumes.
2. The following discussion of Voegelin's obscurity relies on Ellis Sandoz's introduction to *Eric Voegelin's Significance for the Modern Mind* (Baton Rouge, La.: Louisiana State University Press, 1991). See especially 1–7.
3. A notable exception is Ellis Sandoz, who wrote his Ph.D. dissertation under Voegelin. Sandoz is one of the leading commentators on Voegelin's work and is on the editorial board of *The Collected Works of Eric Voegelin.* He is also the series editor for the recently published *History of Political Ideas.* Voegelin cultivated students throughout his professional career, especially while professor and director of the Institute for Political Science, a position at the University of Munich. For Voegelin's reasons for leaving the U.S. and accepting a position in Germany, as well as his view of students in both the U.S. and Europe, see *AR*, 91–92.
4. For a discussion of the *New York Times* and Voegelin's work see George A. Panichas, "The New York Times and Eric Voegelin," *Modern Age* 29 (spring 1985): 98–103.
5. See *New York Times* 23 January 1985, 8(B).

6. Among the enumerated convictions were "[t]hat God's order in man's world includes a moral code, based upon man's unchanging nature and not subject to man's repeal, suspension or amendment." The article also cited Supreme Court Justice Douglas's statement from *Zorach v. Clauson* (1952) that "we are a religious people whose institutions presuppose a Supreme Being," and added that "American history cannot be understood or correct policy formed except with recognition of that fact." Based on this understanding of American political institutions *Time* asserted that "equality before the law is based on each man's dignity in God's sight; that political liberty is based on the soul's freedom to accept or reject the good. . . ." The article suggested that rights must be protected but that the state has an obligation "to protect its authority." In support of this idea, Justice Jackson's comment that the Bill of Rights is not a suicide pact was quoted. Voegelin quotes the very same comment in *The New Science of Politics* and in his essay "Democracy in the New Europe" in *PE 1953–1965*, 59. The final noteworthy conviction was "[t]hat all attempts, revolutionary or reformist, of progress based on the idea that man is perfectible, will lead to stagnation at best and calamity at worst." "Journalism and Joachim's Children," *Time*, 9 March 1953, 57–61.
7. For a lucid discussion of gnosticism and its political implications, see Voegelin, "Gnostic Politics," in *PE 1940–1952*, 223–240.
8. *Time*, 30 March 1953, 6. A gentleman from Minot, North Dakota, wrote "Garbled nonsense. . . . This Voegelin is just another egghead. . . ." Another reader took offense at *Time*'s disparaging portrayal of Comte and stated, "Come on, Time, dig the cultural concept and a little bit of the scientific method if you want to play in the intellectual big leagues. You and Reinhold Niebuhr are sticking your heads into the same sandpile and waving your tailfeathers while the world goes by." *Time*, 23 March 1953, 10.
9. *Time*, 23 March 1953, 10; 30 March 1953, 4.
10. He explained in *AR*: "I have in my files documents labeling me a communist, a Fascist, a National Socialist, an old Liberal, a new Liberal, a Jew, a Catholic, a Protestant, a Platonist, a neo-Augustinian, a Thomist, and of course a Hegelian—not to forget that I was strongly influenced by Huey Long" (46).
11. The attempt to place Voegelin in a particular ideological or political category continues to be evident in recent reviews of his works and in reviews of secondary literature on Voegelin. See, for example, Theodore Weber's review of *Eric Voegelin and the Good Society*, by John J. Ranieri, in

Theological Studies 58 (June 1997): 379–380.

12. George H. Nash considers *The New Science of Politics* to be "one of the most important books by postwar intellectuals of the Right." See Nash, *The Conservative Intellectual Movement in America* (Wilmington, Del.: Intercollegiate Studies Institute, 1996), 42.
13. When Voegelin refers to experience, he means something specific. By experience he means the individual's attunement to the ground of being.
14. Jürgen Gebhardt, Epilogue to *In Search of Order* (Columbia, Mo.: University of Missouri Press, 2000), 131.
15. The term "modern" as it is used by Voegelin and other critics of modernity does not mean simply recent or contemporary. It is a concept with ideological content. As Russell Kirk explains, it means "preference for change over permanence; exaltation of the present era over all previous epochs; hearty approval of material aggrandizement and relative indifference toward a moral order; positive hostility, often, toward theism." Russell Kirk, "Obdurate Adversaries of Modernity," *Modern Age* 31 (summer/fall 1987): 203.
16. See also Voegelin, "On Readiness to Rational Discussion," in *Freedom and Serfdom: An Anthology of Western Thought*, ed., Albert Hunold (Dordrecht, Holland: D. Reidel Publishing Company, 1961): 269–284.
17. See chapter 5 in *FER* for Voegelin's use of these terms.
18. What Voegelin means by the modern or Western crisis will be discussed in detail in chapter 2. A valuable source for understanding the Western crisis is the Thirtieth Anniversary Issue of *Modern Age*, 31 (summer/fall 1987). The theme of the issue is "Essays on the Crisis of Modernity," and it contains several essays on Voegelin or that relate to his understanding of the Western crisis.
19. The frustration readers experience with Voegelin's terminology can be minimized by consulting secondary literature on Voegelin. See, for example, Eugene Webb, *Eric Voegelin: Philosopher of History* (Seattle: University of Washington Press, 1981). Webb provides a useful glossary that includes terms commonly found in Voegelin's writings. This glossary is a starting point for new readers of Voegelin. I have also included a glossary in this book.
20. Gebhardt, Epilogue to *In Search of Order*, 130.
21. For Voegelin's misgivings regarding dogma see "Response to Professor Altizer" (*PE 1966–1985*, 294–295). For his more positive statements about dogma see Webb, *Eric Voegelin: Philosopher of History*, 214.
22. Voegelin is not alone in reaching this conclusion. Leo Strauss and Irving

Babbitt also identify modern methods of analysis, like positivism, as obstacles to the open search for the truth of existence.

23. Voegelin explains in the context of analyzing Plato's *Republic*, "Concerning the content of the Agathon nothing can be said at all. . . . The transcendence of the Agathon makes immanent propositions concerning its content impossible. The vision of the Agathon does not render a material rule of conduct, but forms the soul through an experience of transcendence" (*OH III*, 166–167).
24. For a discussion of Voegelin's analysis of Christianity, see Webb, *Eric Voegelin: Philosopher of History*, 211–236; Also Thomas W. Heilke, *Eric Voegelin: In Quest of Reality* (Lanham, Md.: Rowman & Littlefield Publishers, 1999), 145–177.

Chapter 1

1. For more detailed information on Voegelin's Austrian experience, see Erika Weinzierl's "Historical Commentary on the Period" in volume 4 of *The Collected Works of Eric Voegelin* (*The Authoritarian State*).
2. Sandoz describes Voegelin's Ph.D. dissertation: "It dealt with the ontological problem of the difference between constructing social theory on the assumption of reciprocal relations among autonomous individuals or on the assumption of a preexistent spiritual bond among human beings that would be realized in their interpersonal relations, i.e., the difference between Simmel's individualistic and Spann's universalistic theories of community." Ellis Sandoz, *The Voegelinian Revolution: A Biographical Introduction* (Baton Rouge, La.: Louisiana State University Press, 1981), 38.
3. For the intellectual influences at the University of Vienna that were part of Voegelin's experience as a graduate student and professor in the 1920s, see Sandoz, *The Voegelinian Revolution*, 34–47.
4. Sandoz, *The Voegelinian Revolution*, 40.
5. For more details on Voegelin's American experience, see *AR*, chapter 10, "American Influence," 28–33. See also Sandoz, *The Voegelinian Revolution*, chapter 1.
6. Voegelin provides an extensive critique of Kelsen's pure theory of law and neo-Kantian methodology in *AS*, 163–212.
7. For Voegelin's epistemology, see Charles Warren Burchfield and Patrick Neal Fuller, "The Role of Faith and Love in Voegelin's Mystical Epistemology," *Humanitas* IX, no. 1 (1996): 35–51.

8. A brief representation of Voegelin's analysis of the race problem is found in "The Growth of the Race Idea," (*PE 1940–1952*, 27–61).
9. For a more detailed description of Voegelin's escape from Austria, see Barry Cooper, *Eric Voegelin and the Foundation of Modern Political Science* (Columbia, Mo.: University of Missouri Press, 1999): 1–32.
10. *The Collected Works of Eric Voegelin*, ed. Manfred Henningsen, vol. 5, *Modernity Without Restraint* (Columbia, Mo.: University of Missouri Press, 2000), 1. Voegelin used Thomas Mann as an example of the intellectual failure to critically and spiritually understand the spiritual emptiness of intellectuals in Germany. See "The German University and German Society," (*PE 1966–1985*, 4–5).
11. Ellis Sandoz, "Truth and the Experience of Epoch in History: A Voegelinian Perspective," *Modern Age* 38 (fall 1995): 9.
12. Critics of Voegelin, like David Walsh, consider this aspect of his work to be questionable and Voegelin's argument to be overstated. Walsh attributes Voegelin's depreciation of liberalism to his overstatement of the commonality between liberalism and totalitarianism. Voegelin's argument can be seen as one reason why political and intellectual conservatives find his work appealing. The rise of the welfare state has been condemned by conservatives because it results in the destruction of private and sectional groups and associations that are considered vital to liberty and community. They have also seen the rise of big government as a movement toward totalitarianism. See, for example, Hayek's *Road to Serfdom* or Nisbet's *The Quest for Community*. What may be at the bottom of Walsh's criticisms of Voegelin is ultimately a significantly different political intuition.
13. Sandoz, "Truth and the Experience of Epoch in History: A Voegelinian Perspective," 11.
14. These lectures have been published as volume 31 of *The Collected Works of Eric Voegelin* (*Hitler and the Germans*) (Columbia, Mo.: University of Missouri Press, 1999).
15. Readers who tend to be more interested in history and politics may find works like *Hitler and the Germans* to be more interesting than Voegelin's later work on the philosophy of consciousness.
16. See, for example, the essays in volume 12 (*Published Essays 1966–1985*) of *The Collected Works of Eric Voegelin.*
17. Robert Heilman, *The Professor and the Profession* (Columbia, Mo.: University of Missouri Press, 1999), 85–102.

18. George A. Panichas, "*The New York Times* and Eric Voegelin," *Modern Age* 29 (spring 1985): 103.
19. Lewis P. Simpson, "Voegelin and the Story of the Clerks," in *Eric Voegelin's Significance for the Modern Mind*, ed. Ellis Sandoz (Baton Rouge, La.: Louisiana State University Press, 1991), 71.
20. Gerhart Niemeyer, "Greatness in Political Science: Eric Voegelin (1901–1985)," *Modern Age* 29 (spring 1985): 109.
21. Sandoz, *The Voegelinian Revolution*, 88.
22. See James W. Tuttleton, "T. S. Eliot and the Crisis of the Modern," *Modern Age* 31 (summer/fall 1987): 275–283.
23. One of the more interesting comparisons of Voegelin and another thinker on the Western crisis is provided by Russell Nieli's essay, "The Cry Against Nineveh: Whittaker Chambers and Eric Voegelin on the Crisis of Western Modernity," *Modern Age* 31 (summer/fall 1987): 267–274.
24. For Voegelin's analysis of Scotus Erigena see *HPI IV* (*Renaissance and Reformation*), 151–157.

Chapter 2

1. Speech by Rosalynn Carter to the National Press Club, 20 June 1978.
2. Examples of editorials reacting to Solzhenitsyn's speech are reprinted in Ronald Berman, *Solzhenitsyn at Harvard* (Washington, D.C.: Ethics and Public Policy Center, 1980), 23–29.
3. An example of such a thinker is Hannah Arendt. See Voegelin's review of *The Origins of Totalitarianism* (*PE 1953–1965*, 15–23).
4. Voegelin points out that liberal progressivism and totalitarian ideologies like communism share the same intellectual tradition and are in fact different points on the same ideological continuum. He explains that "one should not deny the immanent consistency and honesty of [the] transition from liberalism to communism; if liberalism is understood as the immanent salvation of man and society, communism certainly is its most radical expression; it is an evolution that was already anticipated by John Stuart Mill's faith in the ultimate advent of communism for mankind" (*NSP*, 175). In another context he writes that "people are shocked by the horrors of war and by Nazi atrocities but are unable to see that these horrors are no more than a translation, to the physical level, of the spiritual and intellectual horrors which characterize progressive civilization in its 'peaceful' phase" (*OH III*, 202 n 4).

5. One might add to Voegelin's distinction that the division also includes the one between true and false transcendentalists.
6. On cultural literacy, see E. D. Hirsch, Jr., *Cultural Literacy* (Boston: Houghton Mifflin, 1987). On our dysfunctional social and political institutions, see James MacGregor Burns, *The Deadlock of Democracy* (Englewood Cliffs, N.J.: Prentice Hall, 1967); Arthur M. Schlesinger Jr., *The Imperial Presidency* (New York: Houghton Mifflin, 1973). Voegelin emphasizes that the crisis is not primarily one of social and political institutions in his review of Hannah Arendt's *The Origins of Totalitarianism* (*PE 1953–1965*, 15).
7. Moulakis, Editor's Introduction (*HPI I*, 54–55).
8. Voegelin defines "pseudological speculation" as having three elements: "(1) that speculation of this kind is theory in appearance only, not in reality; (2) that in the intention of the thinker who indulges in it, it is meant as genuine theoretical speculation; (3) that historically it presupposes the existence of a genuine philosophy of the *logos* which furnishes the subject matter that can be translated into the pseudological form" (*FER*, 264).

Chapter 3

1. Morstein-Marx was a political scientist whom Voegelin met at Harvard. See *AR*, 62–69, for the story of the *History of Political Ideas* project and why Voegelin abandoned it.
2. *A History of Political Theories: Ancient and Medieval* (1902), *A History of Political Theories, from Luther to Montesquieu* (1905), and *A History of Political Theories, from Rousseau to Spencer* (1920).
3. Sabine's text is largely expository and is written from the perspective of "social relativism" (preface to first edition). It focuses on the relationship between political thought and political institutions. It does not analyze the evolution of political ideas by relating them to human participation in transcendent reality. Nor does it provide insights into the connections between existential and political order. This is not surprising given Sabine's own description of his intellectual orientation. Sabine describes his "philosophical preferences" as being consistent with Hume's criticism of natural law: "it is impossible by any logical operation to excogitate the truth of any allegation of fact, and neither logic nor fact implies a value" (preface to first edition). Values are merely creations of "human preferences" in a specific social and physical setting. Given Sabine's approach to the history of

political theory it is no wonder that Voegelin was interested in producing a rival text. Sabine's book has no animating philosophical or diagnostic force other than the provision of an encyclopedic account of the history of political theory.

4. Voegelin's assessment of twentieth-century works of the history of political theory is addressed in "Political Theory and the Pattern of General History" (*PE 1940–1952*, 157–167).
5. Sandoz, *The Voegelinian Revolution*, 76–77.
6. Parts of the *History of Political Ideas* were published as articles. *From Enlightenment to Revolution* appears as volume 26 (*Crisis and the Apocalypse of Man*) in *The Collected Works of Eric Voegelin.*
7. Voegelin's rejection of an approach to history that focuses on the development and evolution of constitutionalism is reflected in his disparaging remark that "A convention has been established, especially in the historiography of 'political ideas,' to ignore the far-flung concerns of the classic philosophy of order and to replace them with the restricted interests of modern constitutionalism" (*OH II*, 98–99). To a degree this statement represents a rejection of Voegelin's own study of the history of political ideas.
8. In this passage Voegelin attributes to tradition an arbitrary characteristic that indicates, in part, why he refused the label "conservative" or "traditionalist." He seems to discount the possibility that tradition can effectively embody the universal. He fails to make qualitative distinctions among traditions, e.g., those that merely mask the *libido dominandi* and those that reflect experience with transcendent reality.
9. As Voegelin would later explain, differentiation runs the risk of derailment and deformation. A more luminous understanding of reality is not a guarantee that political and social life will be ordered accordingly.
10. Of course, that someone like Pope John Paul II speaks of "social justice" does not necessarily mean that he is spiritually corrupt. But Voegelin's contention would be that such language has behind it an ideologically formed state of consciousness that is inconsistent with the genuine spirituality the Pope is trying to convey. That the Pope would use the language of "social justice" and related terms indicates the extent of the Western crisis. He may not intend the ideological meaning of such terms, but they nevertheless tend to evoke the state of spiritual disorder that produced them.

Chapter 4

1. Voegelin argued in his essay "Necessary Moral Bases for Communication in a Democracy" that "[t]he range of theoretical possibilities to find substitutes for the *summum bonum* is, on principle, exhausted" (*PE 1953–1965*, 57).
2. The following analysis of scientism is based on Michael P. Federici, "Logophobia," *The Intercollegiate Review* 35 (fall 1999): 14–21. Voegelin uses the terms "scientism" and "positivism" interchangeably.
3. See, for example, Bacon's *New Atlantis* (1627).
4. Voegelin refers to this revolutionary aspect of positivism as an "apostatic revolt." There is the sense in the positivistic mind that a new order is emerging and that it will replace the existing order. In the historical context in which positivism develops, the apostatic revolt means the displacement of Christianity by modern ideologies. See *HPI VI*, 9–14.
5. In this context Voegelin explains that "Comte belongs, with Marx, Lenin, and Hitler, to the series of men who would save mankind and themselves by divinizing their particular existence and imposing its law as the new order of society. The satanic Apocalypse of Man begins with Comte and has become the signature of the Western crisis" (*FER*, 159).
6. Note, as an example, Comte's transformation of Christian love into altruism. See Voegelin, *From Enlightenment to Revolution* (Durham, N.C.: Duke University Press, 1975), 155; and Voegelin, *Science, Politics and Gnosticism* (Chicago: Regnery Gateway, 1968), 85.
7. Comte refuses to participate in the search for the ground of existence. In Voegelin's framework, he rejects aetiology.
8. In the case of Comte and later positivists, transcendent symbols are replaced or given a new immanentized meaning. See note 6.
9. Voegelin not only gives primacy to experience over method but he gives primacy to experience over doctrine and dogma. In the latter case, the content of doctrine and dogma may deal with transcendent reality but for the same reason that Voegelin rejects positivism he rejects propositional expressions of reality; they both inhibit the open search for the truth of existence. In rejecting positivism and dogmatism, Voegelin was criticized by one side for embracing religious and philosophical truth (and thus not being sufficiently scientific) and by the other side for not fully accepting religious doctrines (and thus not being sufficiently religious).

10. A term used by Heraclitus to signify the common part of human nature that links humans to the transcendent and forms the substance of community.
11. For Voegelin's discussion of ideology and rational debate, see, "On Readiness to Rational Discussion," in *Freedom and Serfdom*, 269–84. Also see Voegelin, "On Debate and Existence," in *The Collected Works of Eric Voegelin*, ed. Ellis Sandoz, vol. 12, *Published Essays: 1966–1985* (Baton Rouge, La.: Louisiana State University Press, 1990), 36–51.
12. In another context Voegelin comments that, "Among the most exasperating experiences I had in the years 1933–1938 were occasional calls by Englishmen, nice liberal Laborites, who could not restrain their indignation at the vile, undemocratic methods used by the Austrian government against such charming innocents as Communists and National Socialists, who were not permitted to organize for the overthrow of the government and even were hampered in their propaganda for this perfectly legitimate undertaking" (*PE 1940–1952*, 22). Voegelin's view contrasts with the one expressed by Justice Holmes in his dissenting opinion in *Gitlow v. New York* (1925). Holmes writes that, "If in the long run the beliefs expressed in proletarian dictatorship are destined to be accepted by the dominant forces of the community, the only meaning of free speech is that they should be given their chance and have their way."
13. Voegelin's five-volume work, *Order and History*, is a recovery of experiences with transcendence. Each volume describes and provides specific examples from history of human participation in transcendent reality.
14. See Barry Cooper, *Eric Voegelin*.
15. See also Voegelin, "Industrial Society in Search of Reason" (*PE 1953–1965*, 178–190).
16. The need for certainty about the meaning of existence is caused in part by Christian differentiation. For Christians the "thread of faith, on which hangs all certainty regarding divine, transcendent being, is indeed very thin. Man is given nothing tangible. The substance and proof of the unseen are ascertained through nothing but faith, which man must obtain by the strength of his soul. . . . Not all men are capable of such spiritual stamina . . . . The reality of being as it is known in its truth by Christianity is difficult to bear, and the flight from clearly seen reality to gnostic constructs will probably always be a phenomenon of wide extent in civilizations that Christianity has permeated" (*SPG*, 109).
17. For Voegelin's understanding of gnostic ideology and rational debate see

Voegelin, "On Debate and Existence," "On Readiness to Rational Discussion," and Sandoz, "Voegelin Read Anew: Political Philosophy in the Age of Ideology," *Modern Age*, XVII (summer 1973): 257–263.

18. The concept of a "leap in being" designates experiences that are characterized by the movement of divine presence as the formative substance of history and order that moves human understanding to a new level of clarity.
19. Voegelin makes this point emphatically in "History and Gnosis" in his rejection of the thesis of Rudolf Bultmann that the Old Testament is theologically irrelevant to Christians. "From the fact that a truth has been differentiated through a new experience it does not follow that everything else known as true in the more compact experience has now become untrue" (*PE 1953–1965*, 173).
20. This is why Voegelin ranks Cicero so low as a philosopher. There is not much philosophical depth to his work and he is more interested in validating the virtues of Rome. Consequently, he fails to provide a paradigm of right order that can serve as both a contrast to the existing political order and a model for members of Roman society to follow.
21. Related to the issue of Augustine's distinction between sacred and profane history is whether or not both Augustine and Voegelin, in following such a view of history, separate transcendence from history and politics too radically. This issue will be addressed in chapter 7. See Shadia B. Drury, "Augustinian Radical Transcendence: Sources of Political Excess," *Humanitas* XII, no. 2 (1999): 27–45.
22. Voegelin's view of modern ideologies and their rejection of a fixed human nature has much in common with the conservatism of Russell Kirk. See Kirk, ed., *The Portable Conservative Reader* (New York: Penguin Books, 1982), xvii–xviii. See, also, Kirk, *The Conservative Mind: From Burke to Eliot* (Washington, D.C.: Regnery Publishing, 1985).
23. Eric Voegelin, "Reading the *Republic*," A panel discussion with Allan Bloom, Hans-Georg Gadamer, Eric Voegelin, and Frederick Lawrence at York University, Toronto (23 November 1978). Voegelin's insistence that Plato was not a utopian contrasts with William Dunning's view of Plato. See Dunning, *A History of Political Ideas: Ancient and Mediaeval* (New York: Macmillan, 1902): 43–47.
24. This does not, however, discount the possibility that Plato is an idealist, which is something short of being a utopian.

Chapter 5

1. *Republic* 561 b–d and 586 a–b are examples.
2. For a more extensive discussion of Voegelin's philosophy of history, see Eugene Webb, *Eric Voegelin: Philosopher of History* (Seattle: University of Washington Press, 1981); and Voegelin, "Configurations of History," in *Collected Works* vol. 12, *PE 1966–1985,* 95–114.
3. Athanasios Moulakis, editor's introduction to *HPI I* (*Hellenism, Rome, and Early Christianity*), 43.
4. For an analysis of the historical antecedents of the American political and social order by a scholar who was influenced by Voegelin's work, see Russell Kirk, *The Roots of American Order* (Washington, D.C.: Regnery Gateway, 1991).
5. Voegelin notes, "History as the form in which a society exists has the tendency to expand its realm of meaning so as to include all mankind—as inevitably it must, if history is the revelation of the way of God with man. History tends to become world-history, as it did on this first occasion in the Old Testament, with its magnificent sweep of the historical narrative from the creation of the world to the fall of Jerusalem" (*OH I*, 169–170).
6. Voegelin believed that "there are times when the divinely willed order is humanly realized nowhere but in the faith of solitary sufferers" (*OH I*, 519).

Chapter 6

1. An interesting work that addresses the relevance of Voegelin's work to questions of order is John J. Ranieri, *Eric Voegelin and the Good Society* (Columbia, Mo.: University of Missouri Press, 1995).
2. Eugene Webb points out that Voegelin is inconsistent in dating the historical boundaries of the Ecumenic Age. See Webb, *Eric Voegelin: Philosopher of History* (Seattle: University of Washington Press), 249, n 13.
3. Voegelin also discusses space exploration in "World Empire and the Unity of Mankind" (*PE 1953–1965*, 140–141).
4. See *OH V*, 58–59 and chapter 2.
5. Voegelin, "Structures in Consciousness," Lecture delivered at York University, Toronto (23 November 1978). The lecture has been transcribed by Zdravko Planinc and is available at: *http://vaz2.concordia.ca/~vorenews/v-rnll3.html.*

Chapter 7

1. See chapter 3.
2. For an analysis of the similarities and differences between Voegelin and Strauss, see Ted V. McAllister, *Revolt Against Modernity: Leo Strauss, Eric Voegelin, and the Search for a Postliberal Order* (Lawrence, Kans.: University Press of Kansas, 1996).
3. David Walsh, *The Growth of the Liberal Soul* (Columbia, Mo.: University of Missouri Press, 1997), 99.
4. Ibid., 100.
5. Ibid., 164.
6. For a discussion of Voegelin and conservatism see Gerhart Niemeyer, "Eric Voegelin 1952," *Modern Age* 26 (summer/fall 1982): 262–266; and George H. Nash, *The Conservative Intellectual Movement in America* (Wilmington, Del.: Intercollegiate Studies Institute, 1996).
7. For Voegelin's characterization of conservatism as an outgrowth of liberalism, see "Liberalism and Its History" (*PE 1953–1965*, 86–87).
8. For Voegelin's comments on conservative skepticism, see *OH II*, 382–383.
9. Examples of nonideological conservatives are Edmund Burke and Russell Kirk.
10. For Voegelin on Sextus Empiricus, see *OH III*, 424–428 and "Immortality: Experience and Symbol" (*PE 1966–1985*, 55).
11. For the continuity of Kirk and Voegelin, see Kirk, *Enemies of the Permanent Things* (La Salle: Sherwood Sugden & Company, 1984).
12. For an analysis of value-centered historicism, see Claes G. Ryn, "Universality and History." *Humanitas* vi, no. 1 (fall 1992/winter 1993): 10–39.
13. The moral abstractness of Voegelin's political philosophy is discussed in Claes G. Ryn, "The Politics of Transcendence: The Pretentious Passivity of Platonic Idealism," *Humanitas* xii, no. 2 (1999): 4–26, and Shadia B. Drury, "Augustinian Radical Transcendence: Sources of Political Excess," *Humanitas* xii, no. 2 (1999): 27–45.
14. Ellis Sandoz takes up the question of Voegelin and conservatism in *The Politics of Truth and Other Untimely Essays: The Crisis of Civic Consciousness* (Columbia, Mo.: University of Missouri Press, 1999). See chapter 9: "Eric Voegelin a Conservative?" Sandoz tends to downplay the conservative side of Voegelin's political writings and overstate the apolitical or nonideological characteristic of his more scholarly work. Sandoz writes that "His thought and almost all of his work move at several removes from the level of political

debate we vaguely reference with our conservative/liberal labels and dichotomy" (139). The conservative side of Voegelin's work is clearly evident in the volume of essays edited by Sandoz, *Published Essays 1953–1965* (Columbia, Mo.: University of Missouri Press, 2000) and in works like *Science, Politics and Gnosticism* and *The New Science of Politics*. Sandoz does admit that "there is rightly enough something strongly conserving about Voegelin's work" (140).

15. For the development and recovery of transcendent symbols and experiences, see Irving Babbitt, Leo Strauss, Russell Kirk, Albert Camus.
16. Stephen J. Tonsor, "The God Question," review of *Eric Voegelin, Published Essays, 1966–1985: The Collected Works of Eric Voegelin, Volume 12*, edited with an introduction by Ellis Sandoz, in *Modern Age* 35 (fall 1992): 67.
17. For Cicero's contribution to ordered liberty, natural law, and justice, see Russell Kirk, *The Roots of American Order* (Washington, D.C.: Regnery Gateway, 1991), 106–113.
18. Voegelin insists that Plato is a moral realist and that the best polis is not an ideal in the sense of a utopian construction. See Voegelin, "Reading the *Republic*," a panel discussion with Allan Bloom, Hans-George Gadamer, Eric Voegelin, and Frederick Lawrence at York University, Toronto (23 November 1978).
19. Voegelin is especially realistic when discussing constitutional government and the ethical limits of democracy. This realism is evident in his essay "Freedom and Responsibility in Economy and Democracy," in which he attributes Germany's totalitarian fall, in part, to German pietism. Specifically he cites the "pietistic trait" to "insulate an existence understood as Christian from the profane, impure sphere of the political" (*PF 1953–1965*, 72). He criticizes the nineteenth-century figure Friedrich Christoph Schlosser, who "popularized the dictum 'power is evil'" (73). He then contrasts Schlosser's view to Lord Acton's dictum "Power corrupts; absolute power corrupts absolutely." Voegelin finds Acton's view of power superior because it represents a more realistic view of power and ethics. In Acton's view is the idea that "power itself is morally neutral—one can use it for better or for worse—but it is always a temptation for man, which is, after all, in accordance with his nature" (73). Voegelin also invokes Alexander Hamilton's view that "men are rascals," and he agrees that a "healthy cynicism" helps ensure that political leaders are sufficiently checked and restrained. He concludes the point by stating that "the pietistic propensity to keep out of

politics because power is evil and politics is a dirty business verges in a democracy on high treason" (74).

20. Tonsor, "The God Question," 66. The following analysis of Voegelin and Christianity is based on Michael P. Federici, "Voegelin's Christian Critics," *Modern Age* 36 (summer 1994): 331–340.
21. Ibid., 68.
22. The first three volumes of *Order and History,* as well as comments in his essays, seemed to suggest that the Christian experience provided the ultimate meaning of history. In analyzing Augustine and Aquinas, for example, Voegelin did not dispute the implication of their view of history: "History is Christ written large" (*PE 1966–1985*, 78).
23. Bruce Douglass, "A Diminished Gospel: A Critique of Voegelin's Interpretation of Christianity," in *Eric Voegelin's Search for Order in History,* ed. Stephen A. McKnight (Baton Rouge, La.: Louisiana State University Press, 1978), 149.
24. Gerhart Niemeyer, "Eric Voegelin's Philosophy and the Drama of Mankind," *Modern Age* 20 (winter 1976): 35.
25. Douglass, "The Gospel and Political Order: Eric Voegelin on the Political Role of Christianity," *The Journal of Politics* 38 (February 1976): 27, 33–37 (emphasis in original).
26. Douglass, "A Diminished Gospel," 146.
27. Marion Montgomery, "Eric Voegelin and the End of Our Exploring," *Modern Age* 23 (summer 1979): 234.
28. Ibid., 243.
29. Ibid., 238.
30. James L. Wiser, "From Cultural Analysis to Philosophical Anthropology: An Examination of Voegelin's Concept of Gnosticism," *The Review of Politics* 42 (January 1980): 99.
31. Ibid., 102, 100, 103.
32. John Hallowell, "Existence in Tension: Man in Search of His Humanity," in *Eric Voegelin's Search for Order in History* (Baton Rouge, La.: Louisiana State University Press, 1978), 125.
33. Hallowell, "Existence in Tension," 126, 123 (emphasis in original).
34. Weatherby, "Myth, Fact, and History," *Modern Age* 22 (spring 1978):148–149 (emphasis in original).

GLOSSARY

A

Agathon. The highest good. Equivalent to *summum bonum* (the greatest good). It is important to contrast the idea of a "higher" good with the modern concept of a "public good" or "public interest." The latter tends to be understood as a mere secular (intramundane) and utilitarian formulation (often confined to material wants) of aggregate self-interest for the greatest number of individuals rather than the idea of attunement to a transcendent moral order.

Aition. The ground of being; the One.

Aletheia. Truth in the sense of experiential truth. It can also be used to mean "reality."

Amor Dei. Love of God (Augustine). The spirit that characterizes the open soul.

Amor Sui. Love of self (Augustine). The spirit that characterizes the closed soul.

Anamnesis. Recollection; the recalling of past experiences that have become dormant in consciousness. Important concept to Voegelin's notion of recovery of experience.

Apeiron. A pole of the structure of reality (*metaxy*) that indicates the origin or beginning of existence and living things. Voegelin locates the *apeiron* as the opposite pole of existence to the Beyond (*epekeina*).

Aphoristic Style. A style of analysis by which the thinker preserves in his ideas the connection between the experiences and sentiments that engender the ideas. Helvétius is an example. This style and the thinkers who use it are important to Voegelin's analysis of the Western crisis because subsequent thinkers often separate their ideas from the original engendering experiences and sentiments. Once separated it is more difficult to trace the ideas back to the experiences and sentiments that inspired them. Evaluating ideas requires assessing the quality of the experiences and sentiments that engender them.

Apostatic Revolt. The rejection of the existing spiritual order and its replacement by a new radically different spiritual order. Positivism's rejection of Christianity is an example of apostatic revolt. Voegelin refers to the new spiritual order as a "counterreligion."

Arche. Origin.

Aristotelian Method/Procedure. To examine language symbols as they occur in reality as opposed to inventing symbols or concepts to explain and analyze reality. Voegelin believes that from the self-interpretative symbols existing in a society the political philosopher can begin to uncover the "little world of meaning" created by a given society. Once identified, these symbols and their corresponding experiences of order can be compared to the political philosopher's understanding of order gained from philosophical insight.

Articulation of Experience. The symbolic expression of experience that takes the form of myth, revelation, history, and philosophy. The expression of experiential reality is intended to uncover the truth of existence, which has universal importance and applications to social, political, and existential order.

Attunement. The ordering of the soul to the Agathon. The orienting of the soul to the ground can be described as following the "voices of conscience and grace in human existence itself" (*OH I,* 42–43).

B

Biondo, Flavio. Fifteenth-century thinker who divided history into ancient, medieval, and modern. He, like Joachim of Flora, is one of the first modern thinkers to demonstrate a consciousness of epoch and to consider himself the representative of a new truth. He is an early figure in the development of modern gnosticism.

Bios Theoretikos. Aristotle's term for the desire for or the life of contemplation. For Aristotle, contemplation is the highest function in man because it develops that part of man that is ultimately divine (*nous*). The contemplative life is the discovery of the divine in man and the participation in the process of immortalization. The classical Greek philosophers believed that the good society was related to the *bios theoretikos*. The life of contemplation was instrumental to setting the tone in society as well as providing philosophical insights regarding truth on which order and justice depended.

Beyond, the. The ultimate part of reality that extends beyond complete human understanding. We are aware of its existence and at the same time aware of our ignorance of it. Equivalent to *epekeina*.

C

Closure. The state of the closed soul, one that lives in rejection of the good; the state of the soul that has refused to search for order. Opposite of open existence. Voegelin uses the term "eclipse" to indicate closure; he also uses terms like "logophobia" and "pneumopathological" to described the closed soul. Gnostics are considered closed because they replace the open search for truth with ideological propositions and doctrines; they attempt to eliminate in consciousness the tension of existence (see egophanic revolt).

Cognitio Fidei. Cognition by faith. Understanding can begin at the more compact level of faith and proceed to the level of reason. Faith directs reason to a more rational and presumably more differentiated understanding of truth.

Compact. Adjective describing symbols and their engendering historical experiences that have, to some degree, uncovered aspects of reality that are present in a meaningful form but have not been recognized as advances that move consciousness beyond the existing level of understanding.

Consciousness of Epoch. A concept that Voegelin uses to describe the idea that a new and final age is beginning and an old one ending. In *FER* he attributes to the Enlightenment a consciousness of epoch that is connected to Joachim of Flora in the thirteenth century. Flavio Biondo is another example of a thinker who has consciousness of epoch because he divided history into ancient, medieval, and modern. The movement, however, does not reach the point of significant political and social revolution until the eighteenth century. The consequence includes the "lost meaning of Christian existence" (*FER*, 5) and the rise of political mass movements.

Constitution of Being, the. The permanent structure of

existence. Given a fixed human condition (*condicio humana*), political and social life are subject to limits that gnostics and other ideologues refuse to accept. Gnosticism is a revolt against the constitution of being because it attempts to transform it. Equivalent to "the order of being," "the structure of reality," and "the human condition."

Consubstantial. The participation of various levels of reality, as for example in the case of *nous* through which both divine and human presence are experienced.

Corpus Mysticum. "The mystical body." Concept developed by St. Paul to signify the community of Christ into which one enters at baptism.

Cosmion. Voegelin's term for the "little world of order" created by a society through its self-interpretative symbols and corresponding experiences. Voegelin borrows the term from the Austrian philosopher Adolf Stöhr. A cosmion acts as a shelter against disorder and decay. Voegelin bases the concept on William James's term "subuniverse." The cosmion is defended and rationalized in a way that produces historical records that can be analyzed to uncover the history of ideas. The cosmion is a reflection of a larger and higher order that implies the need to subordinate human will to transcendent reality. Totalitarian regimes, because they only recognize intramundane reality, substitute the cosmion for the cosmos.

Cosmos. Ordered reality including both its material and

spiritual components. Ironically, contemporary use of the term excludes parts of reality (e.g., *nous*, revelation, grace, philosophy) that Voegelin considers most vital to meaning and order.

Cosmic Analogue. Society understood as a reflection of the larger ordered universe. Societies represent themselves through self-interpretation and institutions analogous to the larger cosmic order. Political rule, for example, involves the task of ordering society in harmony with the larger cosmic order.

Cosmological Symbols. Self-interpretative symbols that consider social and political institutions as representative of the order observable in the cosmos.

D

Deculturation. The loss of culture that results from closure to transcendent experience. The restoration of order through the recovery of engendering experience with transcendent reality is Voegelin's prescriptive response to deculturation.

Deformation. The destruction of the soul by existential closure or ideological corruption. Equivalent to deculturation. Deformation can occur when differentiated truth is deformed into ideological dogmas or doctrines. For example, Marx's notion of "emancipation" is a deformation of the Gospel idea of *metanoia* (genuine spiritual conversion).

Demiurge. Creator of the cosmos.

Derailment. A deviation from an established truth. An example is Nietzsche's concept "force" as a world-immanent replacement for the Christian notion of grace. The term "derailment" Voegelin borrows from Karl Jaspers as a translation of "*Entgleisung.*"

Despiritualization. The relegation of spiritual matters and symbols to private life. Positivism's displacement of Christianity is an example. Despiritualization is followed by respiritualization; Christianity is replaced by modern ideologies that contain a semblance of Christianity but are devoid of its spiritual substance. The Christian virtue of loving one's neighbor, for example, is transformed into the far less ethically strenuous practice of humanitarian altruism or loving mankind in the abstract. This derailment of Christian love "holds a powerful appeal to spiritually and intellectually immature men who can reap the emotional benefits of being members of the tribe in good standing without submitting to the unpleasant discipline of spirit and intellect; when the truth of existence as an obligation for everyman is abolished, one can participate in representative humanity without [moral] effort" (*PE 1953–1965,* 149–150).

Differentiation. The process by which the truth of existence is understood and articulated in a deeper and more complete way. Plato, for example, differentiates transcendent reality as a presence in the soul denoted by such terms as "*nous*" and "*helkein.*" The more compact understanding of transcendence in cosmological societies understood the universal as a power in the cosmos.

Dike. Justice; right order; higher law.

Doctrinalization. The codifying of historical experience into doctrines. Voegelin opposed doctrinalization because he believed that it resulted in the separation of language symbols from their engendering experience and thus it obscured the truth of reality. Likewise doctrinalization leads to the fragmenting of reality because the complexity and fullness of reality cannot be reduced to dogmatic propositions about truth. Voegelin spells it "doctrinization."

Doxa. Opinion as opposed to truth or true knowledge (*episteme*). A philodoxer is a lover of opinion, as opposed to the philosopher, who is a lover of truth and wisdom.

E

Ecumene. The attempt to create a universal community of mankind in either a spiritual or imperial sense. The recognition of and desire to create a worldwide human community has animated imperial conquests throughout the world.

Egophanic Revolt. Voegelin's term to "designate the concentration on the epiphany of the ego as the fundamental experience that eclipses the epiphany of God in the structure of

Classic and Christian consciousness" (*AR*, 67). The revolt is an attempt to remove the tension of existence by transforming it into "a completely resolved possession of wisdom" in the form of doctrine. Voegelin used the equivalent term "apocalypse of man" in the *NSP*. He changed to "egophanic revolt" in the later work of *OH* in order to emphasize the reductionist aspect of gnosticism. "The discovery of man had to be paid for by the death of God, as this phenomenon was called by Hegel and Nietzsche" (*AR*, 67–68).

Elemental Representation. The conventional idea of political representation; representation in the constitutional sense (e.g., U.S. senators are elemental representatives).

Engendering Experience. The historical experiences that inspire the symbolic articulation of the truth of existence. The pervasiveness of ideology in the late modern age compelled Voegelin to address the ideological deformation of symbols. He believes that the confusion caused by the ideological deformation of symbols could only be remedied by invoking the original language symbols that articulate experiential reality. This endeavor required that the original meaning of language symbols that has become opaque be illuminated by the restoration of the engendering experiences that inspired the creation of the symbols.

Epekeina. The beyond; the transcendent.

Episteme. Knowledge; science as opposed to *doxa*.

Equivalence of Experience. Voegelin argued that reality is known to humans in various ways—myth, history, philosophy, revelation. Consciousness of reality occurs in a variety of cultures and historical contexts. The experience with transcendent reality in these various cultural and historical contexts is comparable and sometimes even equivalent. What makes symbols and experiences equivalent is the common reality that they describe. The parousia is the presence of the divine ground that makes one experience equivalent to another and what allows someone living in a particular society and age able to recognize and understand symbols and experiences from other societies and ages.

Eschatology. Speculation about the final and ultimate destiny of man. There is eschatological pathos in Marx because he claims to have discovered the destiny of man as the perfection of human nature in history. Closely related to millenarianism. Utopian and gnostic ideologies like communism and National Socialism believe that it is possible to immanentize the eschaton (bring heaven to earth).

Estrangement. A spiritual condition characterized by closure and revolt against the transcendent ground. Estrangement is a desolation of the spirit (an estrangement from reality) that breeds a spiritual disease Voegelin, following Shelling, calls "pneumopathology." The estranged individual, what Heraclitus calls an "*idiotes*," is alienated from the human community that is formed by *homonoia*, *metanoia*, and grace. Voegelin applies the concept to the rise of Nazi Germany and the postwar period.

Etiology. The examination of the quest (search) for the ground of existence. *Aition* is Greek for "the ground."

Eunomia. Attunement to the transcendent; the spiritual and intellectual order that results from attunement to the divine ground.

Existence in Truth. Open existence. The philosopher's open search for the truth of existence contrasts to the ideologue's or philodoxer's closed existence. Closed existence ends the search for the truth of existence and rests in ideological propositions and doctrinalization.

Existential Representation. Representation of a society in the larger order. Representation of society with regard "to the whole range of human existence, including its spiritual dimension" (*NSP*, 43). Sir John Fortescue is one of the first to understand existential representation. Voegelin explains his initial use of existential representation and what he meant by it in *AR* (64–65).

F

Fragmentizing. The common tendency of ideologues to take a part of reality, reduce it to doctrine or proposition, and consider it the whole of reality. Once fragmentizing occurs, the search for the truth of existence ends; philosophy is replaced by ideology. The claim made by existentialists that "life is absurd" is an example of fragmentizing. Life includes the experience of absurdity but it is one of a variety of human experiences and thus should not be treated as the defining characteristic of human existence.

G

Gnosis. False knowledge that may contain fragments of reality. Distinct from *episteme* because it is not acquired from philosophical analysis but emanates from the vision of an existentially closed soul. This knowledge is used by gnostics to attempt to transform the world by creating a new structure of reality. Marx's idea that the world can be fundamentally reordered without social classes, private property, and government is an example of gnosis.

Gnosticism. An ideology that claims absolute knowledge of reality. It characterizes the modern world according to Voegelin. It is engendered by dissatisfaction with the structure of existence as it is and the belief that a new order can be created by implementing a revolutionary plan of action based on gnosis. The new order represents a transformation of human nature and the very structure of existence.

Ground, the. The ground of existence is the transcendent reality that is experienced as a pull toward the good. The orienting center of life. The open soul is open to the ground in that it attunes itself to the ordering force that emanates from the ground. The pull of the ground is felt by the *psyche*, the sensorium of transcendence.

H

Hebrews 11:1. "Faith is the substance of things hoped for, the evidence of things unseen." In contrast to gnostic thinkers like Hegel and Marx, Voegelin maintains an intellectual humility that recognizes that man's understanding of truth is limited. Consequently, his philosophy of history is written in the spirit of *Hebrews* 11:1.

Helkein. The act of being drawn or pulled by God or the ground of being (e.g., by grace).

Historiogenesis. Speculation on the origin and cause of a society. The term fits in a typology of speculations (e.g., anthropogony: the origin of man; cosmogony: the origin of the cosmos; and theogony: the origin of the gods). Historiogenetic constructions include "enlightened" progressivism, Comtism, Hegelianism, and Marxism.

Historia Sacra. Church history; used by Augustine to distinguish from profane (secular) history.

Homonoia. Term used by Aristotle and others to indicate

"likemindedness" in the sense of spiritual commonality. *Homonoia* is the community-forming substance without which justice and order cannot exist. Hobbes tries to construct a society without *homonoia* and puts in its place mere self-interest and fear.

Hypostatized. The reification of concepts that gives them the status of objects with independent existence.

I

Immanentism. An ideology that conceives of reality as wholly immanent (e.g., positivism).

Immortalizing. Aristotle's notion of orienting the soul to the divine ground.

Instrumentalization of Man. The dehumanization of man by reducing his value and meaning to pleasure, pain, and passion. Man loses his spiritual quality because he is thought to be completely alienated from transcendence.

Intentionality. A structure of consciousness. Describes the part of human consciousness that orients itself toward an "object" like reality.

Intra-Cosmic *vs.* Extra-Cosmic. Voegelin explains that in polytheism the gods are intra-cosmic, i.e., they are part of the cosmos not beyond it. Christianity differentiates an extra-cosmic God who is present in the cosmic world but at the same time transcends it and is the creator of it.

Intramundane. Completely within the realm of immanent reality. Voegelin uses this concept to refer to thinkers and ideas that remove the transcendent from their conception of reality. Hobbes, for example, has an element of intramundane religiousness in his political theory because he replaces the *summum bonum* (greatest good) with the *summum malum* (the greatest evil—fear of violent death). Because genuine order has transcendent roots, intramundane theories of politics ignore basic elements of the truth of existence; they are logophobic. The result of intramundane theories is that society becomes a closed universe with an immanent process of salvation or what Voegelin calls "intraworldly religiousness" (*FER*, 11).

Intramundane Religiousness. A new religiousness which emerges in the Enlightenment and "expresses itself through the inversion of the direction in which the *realissimum* of existence is to be sought" (*FER*, 69). Man is not ordered from above by the loving grace of God but from below by self-interest and utilitarian calculation. This sentiment is present in Hobbes and Helvètius.

Ismic Constructions. Any ideological construction (most of which end with an "ism," e.g., progressivism, Marxism, communism, scientism).

J

Joachim of Fiore (Flora). A twelfth-century Calabrian monk whom Voegelin considers an important figure in the development of modern gnosticism. Joachim created a "consciousness of epoch"—that is, an attitude that suggests that a new and final age has begun, that a new order has replaced the old order. In Joachim's case the old order is Christianity and the new order is a deformation of Christianity. He conceived of history in three epochs giving rise to the very idea of modernity.

K

Kallipolis. The beautiful polis described by Plato in the *Republic* and considered by some to be his ideal regime.

Kinesis. The tension of being moved to search for the truth of existence.

L

Leap in Being. Voegelin's term for progress in the uncovering of the truth of existence. He uses it in the early volumes of *OH* but tends to replace it with "differentiation" in later works. He describes a leap in being as a "qualitative leap" in the discovery of truth rather than an increase of understanding on the same level (*OH I*, 48).

Libido Dominandi. The will to power. A defining characteristic of gnostics, who eventually reveal that behind their ideological propositions lies the lust for power and domination.

Logophobia. Fear and hatred of philosophy; a refusal to engage in the search for the truth of existence. Logophobic thinkers replace the search for truth with ideological propositions. Voegelin identifies logophobia as a defining characteristic of totalitarianism. Marx is an example. Voegelin explains the consequences of philosophical closure by noting that "the prohibition of questions is not harmless, for it has attained great social effectiveness among men who forbid themselves to ask questions in critical situations" (*SPG*, 26).

Logos. Intellect capable of comprehending eternal being; reason. Not all truth is accessible to *logos*.

Luminosity. A structure of consciousness. An important concept in Voegelin's philosophy of consciousness. It describes the process by which humans become aware of reality. Reality becomes luminous to varying degrees. The "It" or "It-reality" becomes luminous in the sense of an individual being aware that he is participating in the process of reality unfolding.

M

Mana. From the Greek word "*dynamis,*" meaning virtue or power. Voegelin explains that "Jesus is possessed of a mana . . .

that he can communicate to other persons and that can start various processes in them, usually healing processes" (*HPI I*, 154).

Mediterranean Tradition. The tradition of classical and Judeo-Christian philosophy represented by such thinkers as Plato, Aristotle, Augustine, and Aquinas. Voegelin argues that the crisis of the West parallels the eclipse of this tradition by modern gnosticism. Restoration of Western civilization depends on the recovery of experiences with transcendence articulated by the representatives of the Mediterranean tradition.

Metalepsis. The participation of both the divine and the human in consciousness.

Metanoia. A change of heart or spiritual conversion. Equivalent to *periagoge*.

Metastatic Apocalypse. The transformation of reality through an act of faith. Voegelin associates the idea of magic with this concept. He developed the concept to describe the Israelite prophets, like Isaiah, who counseled the King of Judah "not to rely on the fortifications for Jerusalem and the strength of his army but on his faith in Yahweh. If the king would have true faith, God would do the rest by producing an epidemic or a panic among the enemy, and the danger to the city would dissolve." The king was smart enough not to follow this advice, but "[s]till, there was the prophet's assumption that through an act of faith the structure of reality could be effectively changed"

(*AR*, 68). This type of consciousness is evident in progressive liberalism.

Metastatic Faith. Metastatic faiths attempt to radically transform being, the structure of reality, itself. These utopian beliefs are escapist in that they suggest that humans can leap out of the *metaxy* and create societies that have found a way to eliminate the tension of existence. The tension or anxiety of existence "is more than a fear of death in the sense of biological extinction; it is the profounder horror of losing, with the passing of existence, the slender foothold in the partnership of being that we experience as ours while existence lasts" (*OH I*, 43). Marxism is a modern example of a metastatic faith. Metastatic faith is one of the primary causes of the Western crisis because it provides the conditions for the rise of ideological mass movements like Nazism and communism.

Metaxy. The permanent in-between structure of existence. Sometimes referred to as the between or in-between, meaning that humans live in a structure of reality that is between the poles of existence (the *Apeiron* and the Beyond).

Myth. A language form common in cosmological societies. It is not engendered by *logos*; it is not an analytical description of reality but a story that conveys a likely truth.

N

Narcissistic Closure. A term used by Voegelin to describe the spiritual condition of a closed soul that revolts against the transcendent ground of being by substituting man for the divine ground. Equivalent to estrangement.

Noesis. The activity of *nous* that differentiates reality.

Noetic Differentiation. The movement in consciousness from compactness to differentiation.

Nomos. Law; convention; right order.

Nosos. Spiritual sickness that breeds injustice.

Nous. Intellect that is a divinely creative substance. It is a point of contact between the human and the divine.

O

Omphalos. Greek term meaning "the navel of the world, at which transcendent forces of being flow into social order" (*OH I*, 67). Point that marks the center of the universe, which joins the political community and the cosmos.

One-line Histories. A concept Voegelin uses to describe the nineteenth-century histories provided by such thinkers as Hegel, Marx, and Comte, who conceived of history as proceeding from "somewhere in a remote antiquity beyond exact knowledge and then advancing towards the great present"

(*CEV*, 113). In each case history is seen as an unfolding of consciousness. But these histories are not verified by "empirical knowledge" of history. Rather than one history that culminates in Western civilization, Voegelin claims there are parallel histories.

Opaque. A term that Voegelin uses to describe language symbols that have lost their original meaning because they have been separated from their engendering historical experience. The opposite of "transparent."

Openness. The philosopher's soul in open search for reality, unencumbered by ideology or pneumopathological disorders. Voegelin's use of the term borrows from Henri-Louis Bergson.

P

Paradox of Modernity. Concomitant progress and decline. The progress is in the area of science and technology, which has led to remarkable levels of material comfort, education, and health. Yet this progress has come at the expense of spiritual decline. Destructive wars, ideologically motivated materialism, and alienation have engendered a body of literature on the decline of the West.

Parousia. The presence of the divine in equivalent human experiences. Its presence in human consciousness and historical experiences allows individuals living in different historical periods and cultures to recognize the same reality in various historical experiences and symbols. It is what gives history its universal quality.

Participation. A term used to describe existence in the structure of reality as a state of participation that includes the consubstantiality of consciousness.

Pathos. The passion and emotion that is associated with human life and the anxiety of the *metaxy*. Voegelin argued that at the level of *pathos* individuals who were open to truth could be educated and turned away from spiritual disorder. Ideological doctrines create a cultural climate that compels the philosopher to appeal to *pathos* as a way of penetrating to the truth of existence that all humans share in experience.

Periagoge. Turning of the soul toward the transcendent ground. This idea of conversion is key to Voegelin's project because it gives it an ethical dimension. Without concrete individuals ordering their souls in accordance with the divine ground, restoration is not possible.

Philodoxy. Love of opinion (*doxa*).

Philosophy. Love of and search for wisdom.

Philosophical Anthropology. Voegelin's view of human nature and its relation to society that relies on the classical and Judeo-Christian understanding of the soul. A belief in original sin and the duality of a soul divided by good and evil inclinations characterizes this traditional view of human nature.

Philosophy of History. The search for meaning in history. In Voegelin's philosophy of history the truth of existence is unfolded through time. Human understanding of history and truth is never complete because the ultimate meaning of history is a mystery. In this regard, Voegelin's philosophy of history can be differentiated from that of Marx and Hegel.

Plato's Anthropological Principle. The interpenetration of existential and social order. This idea is present in Plato's *Republic* where Plato draws connections between the order of the soul and the order of the polis. If the polis is man (the soul) writ large, then political and social order depend on leaders who have attuned their souls to the ground. The degeneration of regimes is ultimately a degeneration of moral character in the ruling class. By implication, political and social institutions are incapable of maintaining a just order without leaders of sound moral character.

Pneuma. The transcendent spirit that moves the soul toward the ground. Equivalent to *helkein.*

Pneumatic Differentiation. The reaction to *pneuma* in the sense of man's response to the divine pull; the understanding of the transcendent as a separate entity from creation.

Pneumopathology. A spiritual disease whose primary symptom is arbitrarily omitting "an element of reality in order to create the fantasy of a new world" (*SPG*, 101).

Primary Experience. Understanding of transcendent presence in the cosmological events of the universe like the change of seasons, tides, and weather, without the differentiation of a personal god present in every man.

Profane History. The category of history that comes out of the Enlightenment and is represented in thinkers like Voltaire. It is distinguished from Augustine's notion of sacred history. With the Enlightenment comes the idea that sacred history is irrelevant to history. Voltaire writes the first universal history but his "empirical completeness" lacks the transcendental universalism found in Augustine. A new universalism is present in Enlightenment-modern histories. The old notion of transcendence is replaced by a "new intraworldly religiousness."

Pseudological Speculation. Nontheoretical speculation—speculation that is closed to aspects of reality because of rigid ideological adherence—by "spiritually diseased" thinkers like Marx.

Psyche. The sensorium of transcendence; "that organ of man by which he experiences or in which he experiences the various tensions" such as love, hope, and faith. Voegelin explains that in so far as the *psyche* "is engaged in" love, hope, and faith, it "can be called 'noetic' self, 'noetic' being derived from *nous*, the Greek term for the intellectual self" (*CEV*, 9).

R

Realissimum. The highest reality. Used to represent the divine ground or transcendent.

Reflective Distance. A structure of consciousness. The recognition of the difference between experiencing reality as a conscious event of participation and expressing that experience symbolically.

Representation. "The form by which a political society gains existence for action in history." Societies use symbols to represent transcendent truth. This is a process of self-interpretation (*NSP*, 1). Voegelin classifies three types of representation: "elemental," "existential," and "transcendental."

S

Sacrum Imperium. A concept from the Middle Ages that derives from the Christian notion of the kingdom of God and evolves into the idea of the Western Christian civilization. Its more literal meaning is "sacred empire."

Scientism. An ideology that subordinates the search for truth to scientific method. Interchangeable with positivism.

Secondary Ideologies. Ideologies like conservatism and traditionalism that are created to preserve the existing order from radical political movements like Jacobinism or Marxism.

Voegelin rejects secondary ideologies because they form ideological propositions to preserve truth but in doing so they risk separating symbols from their engendering experiences and they tend to close off the search for truth. David Hume is an example of a secondary ideologue.

Second Reality. Term used by Voegelin, following Robert Musil and Heimito von Doderer, to denote false perceptions of the human condition. The creation of a second reality is akin to creating an "imaginary reality" that serves the purpose of screening "the first reality of common experience" from human perception. The creation of a second reality is an act of imagination that deceives the self into perceiving life in a way that creates friction between the self and first reality. This friction is the impetus for the revolt against reality that characterizes modern ideological movements.

Self-interpretation. The self-illumination of a society. Voegelin notes that from within particular societies "elaborate symbolism" is used to express the meaning of that society, including its place in history and in the larger reality (cosmos).

Soteriological Symbols. Symbols created to express the experience of being moved by a personal god who exists in the human soul.

Spengler, Toynbee, Jaspers, Hegel. Intellectuals who wrote philosophies of history. Voegelin's work is contrasted to theirs because it does not claim to have discovered the ultimate meaning of history.

Spoudaios. Aristotle's term for the mature man.

Summum Bonum. The greatest or highest good; the transcendent standard of justice and the good. Equivalent to Agathon.

T

Theogonic Process. Term Voegelin borrows from Schelling to describe the "movement of religious sentiment" in profane history.

Theophany. Movement toward the divine that results from attunement. Distinguished from egophany, which is movement away from the divine, a revolt from transcendence.

Transcendent. The universal; the ground of being; the Beyond.

Transcendental Representation. Representation of transcendent truth. Voegelin argues that in addition to existential representation societies represent transcendent truth. "By transcendental representation I meant the symbolization of the governmental function as representative of divine order in the cosmos." In the modern age, the "god whom the government represents has been replaced by an ideology of history that now the government represents in its revolutionary capacity" (*AR*, 65).

Transparent. Voegelin's term for language symbols that have not lost their original meaning because they remain attached to their engendering experiences and thus remain a living force in social and political existence.

Transposition. Voegelin uses this concept to explain how eighteenth-century thinkers like Turgot transpose the Christian idea of mankind. "Turgot's evocation of the *mass totale* transposes the Christian idea of mankind into the utilitarian key." The Christian idea of mankind is that a universal community exists because each human being possesses within the Spirit the divine spark. This part of human nature allows individuals to participate in transcendental reality and thus experience *homonoia*. "This bond of the spirit is timeless" (*FER*, 96). But with Turgot and other modern thinkers, the masses are disconnected from the transcendent. The transposition includes the idea that "intramundane mankind as a whole is the new *realissimum*" and that the intellectual or political leaders of the *masse totale* are god-men (*FER*, 98). Comte, for example, considers himself both the new Messiah and the Pope.

Truth of Existence. Voegelin's term for the "object" of the philosopher's quest.

X

Xynon. The common reality that humans experience (Heraclitus). The common ground to which philosophers, poets, and prophets refer to convey the truth of reality.

Z

Zetema. The intellectual and existential search for truth.

Zetesis. The search for the truth of existence that is engendered by the transcendent pull (*helkein*).

INDEX

X

Z